NOW YOU
KNOW CANADA

NOW YOU KNOW CANADA

150 Years of Fascinating Facts

DOUG LENNOX

DUNDURN
TORONTO

Cover image: 123rf.com/Yulia Ryabokon
Printer: Webcom

Library and Archives Canada Cataloguing in Publication

Lennox, Doug, author
          Now you know Canada : 150 years of fascinating facts / Doug Lennox.

Issued in print and electronic formats.
ISBN 978-1-4597-3942-0 (softcover).--ISBN 978-1-4597-3943-7 (PDF).--
ISBN 978-1-4597-3944-4 (EPUB)

          1. Canada--Miscellanea. I. Title.

FC61.L46 2017   971.002   C2017-901077-8
                                                                  C2017-901078-6

1   2   3   4   5   21   20   19   18   17

  Conseil des Arts   Canada Council
du Canada   for the Arts

We acknowledge the support of the **Canada Council for the Arts** and the **Ontario Arts Council** for our publishing program. We also acknowledge the financial support of the **Government of Ontario**, through the **Ontario Book Publishing Tax Credit** and the **Ontario Media Development Corporation**, and the **Government of Canada**.

Care has been taken to trace the ownership of copyright material used in this book. The author and the publisher welcome any information enabling them to rectify any references or credits in subsequent editions.
                                                              — *J. Kirk Howard, President*

The publisher is not responsible for websites or their content unless they are owned by the publisher.

Printed and bound in Canada.

VISIT US AT

dundurn.com | @dundurnpress | dundurnpress | dundurnpress

Dundurn
3 Church Street, Suite 500
Toronto, Ontario, Canada
M5E 1M2

CONTENTS

O CANADA! 7

POLICY-MAKERS AND GROUND-BREAKERS 17

REBELLIONS 26

CANADA AT WAR 34

HEROES AND LEGENDS 45

PRODIGIES OF SCIENCE, INVENTION, AND MEDICINE 53

CANADIAN DISASTERS 59

INTREPID EXPLORERS 64

ENTERTAIN ME 75

THE OLD BALL GAME 81

GRIDIRON HISTORY 87

CANADA'S GAME 110

THE BEAUTIFUL GAME ... NOW IN CANADA 147

SCOOPS ON CANADIAN HOOPS 151

CANADA'S OTHER NATIONAL GAME 155

ROCKS AND ROLLS 160

MAKING A SPLASH 165

OLYMPIC FEATS 169

MORE CHAMPIONS OF CANADIAN SPORT 181

AFTERWORD 193

QUESTION AND FEATURE LIST 195

O CANADA!

Who gave the word *Canadian* its modern meaning?

In the days of New France, *Canadien* referred to the ancestors of modern French Canadians. After the Treaty of Paris in 1763 transferred New France to the British Crown, and English and Scottish settlers established themselves, the name continued to refer to those of French descent. The first known use of *Canadian* in its modern civic sense, meaning a resident of Canada regardless of ethnicity, dates from the first election to the Assembly of Lower Canada in 1791. The twenty-three-year-old Prince Edward, son of the king and future father of Queen Victoria, who was then a resident in Quebec City, broke up a riot between English and French voters and demanded of them: "Part then in peace. Let me hear no more of the odious distinction of English and French. You are all His Britannic Majesty's beloved Canadian subjects."

DID YOU KNOW ...
that Canada is the second-largest country in the world, covering 9.985 million square kilometres?

What is the official motto of Canada?

Canada's national motto is *A Mari usque ad Mare*, Latin for "From Sea to Sea," which is taken from Psalm 72:8, "And he [the King] shall have dominion also from sea to sea and from the river unto the ends of the earth." The first part of the psalm is inscribed on the Peace Tower (tour de la Paix) in Ottawa.

What does *True North* mean in the English version of the anthem "O Canada"?

- -

True North was borrowed from Alfred, Lord Tennyson's poem in which he refers to Canada as "That True North whereof we lately heard" in reference to its loyalty to Queen Victoria. It does not mean the North Pole or the real north, implying that the northern lands of other countries are false. It is the use of *true* in its other context of meaning loyal or faithful, as, for example, lovers are described as "true to each other." The line of the anthem is describing Canada as loyal to the Crown: "With glowing hearts we see thee rise, / The True North strong and free!"

?

DID YOU KNOW ...
that the highest tides in the world occur in the Bay of Fundy, in New Brunswick, where they peak at around sixteen metres, approximately the height of a five-storey building?

How big is Canada's newest territory?

- -

Nunavut became Canada's third territory in 1999. It is both the least populous and the largest in area of Canada's provinces and territories, taking up one-fifth of Canada's total land area. One of the world's most remote, sparsely settled regions, it has a population of just 37,100, mostly Inuit, living in an area of just over 1,750,000 square kilometres, which is the size of Western Europe.

Other interesting facts about our newest territory: Nunavut is home to the world's northernmost permanently inhabited place, Alert. The Eureka weather station on Ellesmere Island has the lowest average annual temperature of any Canadian weather station. And the motto of Nunavut is *Nunavut Sannginivut*, Inuktitut for "Our land, our strength."

Why are the colours of Canada red and white?

Following the terrible ordeal of the First World War, King George V wished to honour the gallant sacrifice made by his Canadian subjects. He therefore assumed Royal Arms of Canada, and in doing so he assigned red and white as the royal livery colours. Red represented the blood shed by Canadians in the war, and white represented the bandages that were associated with that sacrifice. In later years, when the national flag was adopted, it bore the red and white colours of Canada.

DID YOU KNOW ...

that Canada has two national animals — the beaver and the Canadian horse? The government of Canada passed a bill in 2002 that made the Canadian horse an official symbol and a national animal of Canada. The horse is associated with the agricultural traditions and historical origins of the province of Quebec, and hence, provincial legislation now recognizes the Canadian horse as a "heritage breed of Quebec."

Why was the maple leaf chosen as the national badge of Canada?

The maple leaf became Canada's national badge in direct consequence of the tour of British North America by the Prince of Wales (later King Edward VII) in 1860. It was in that year, during the public planning for the royal tour, that native-born Canadians voiced their desire for a badge to wear when welcoming the prince, to match the English rose, Scottish thistle, Welsh leek, Irish shamrock, or French lily. By general consensus the maple leaf was adopted. Knowing of this the prince brought tableware with him decorated with maple leaves to use on his tour and to present as gifts. Later he gave the maple leaf official recognition as a royal badge by incorporating it into the design for his coronation invitation cards. Subsequently, the maple leaf was introduced into the Royal Arms of Canada and from there into the National Flag.

When was our national anthem "O Canada" first played?

The national anthem was composed by Calixa Lavallée at the request of the St. Jean Baptiste Society. With lyrics by Sir Adolphe-Basile Routhier, "O Canada" was first played at a concert before the Marquis of Lorne, governor general of Canada and son-in-law of Queen Victoria, in Quebec City on June 24, 1880 (St. Jean Baptiste Day).

DID YOU KNOW ...
that Canada has the longest coastline of any country in the world? According to the *Canadian Encyclopedia*, if you include all measurable islands, the saltwater coastline of the country has been measured at 243,797 kilometres in length.

Who were the leading Fathers of Confederation?

Sir John A. Macdonald was unarguably the driving force behind Confederation, and he is still regarded as one of Canada's greatest prime ministers. However, he would not have realized his dream of a Canadian nation had it not been for the efforts of six other men: Thomas D'Arcy McGee of Montreal, one of the most eloquent orators of the time; George Brown of Canada West (Ontario), founder of the *Globe* newspaper; Sir George-Étienne Cartier, political leader of Canada East (Quebec) who believed a united Canada was in the best interests of the Quebecois;

Sir Alexander T. Galt, who represented Anglophones in Canada East; Samuel L. Tilley, premier of New Brunswick; and Charles Tupper, premier of Nova Scotia.

When did Canada officially become its own country?

In 1982, under the leadership of Prime Minister Pierre Trudeau, the Canada Act was passed, repatriating our constitution and ending the necessity for the British Parliament to be involved in order to make changes to the Constitution of Canada. The Canada Act received royal assent on March 29, 1982, in London, but it was not until Queen Elizabeth came to Canada that the Constitution Act, its Canadian equivalent, was proclaimed by letters patent as a statutory instrument by Queen Elizabeth. The Constitution Act was signed into law by Elizabeth II as Queen of Canada on April 17, 1982, on Parliament Hill in Ottawa. Queen Elizabeth's constitutional powers over Canada were not affected by the Canada Act, and she remains queen and head of state of Canada.

How did the city of Calgary get its name?

In 1875, during some troubles with the First Nations, the local North-West Mounted Police (NWMP) sent E Troop under Inspector E.A. Brisebois to erect a barracks on the Bow River. When Brisebois wanted to name the new structure after himself, his commander, Lieutenant-Colonel James Macleod, overruled him and named the settlement Fort Calgary, after the ancestral home of his cousins, the MacKenzies, in Scotland. The Gaelic translation of Calgary is "clear running water," which certainly describes the Bow River. The translation of the Blackfoot name for the area was "elbow many houses." The translated Cree name for the area was "elbow house." Both aboriginal references are to the Elbow River.

How did Niagara Falls get its name?

In 1641, the first reference to the mighty falls was written down as *Onguiaahra*, which is how it sounded in the local dialect, and because the First Nations peoples of the area had no written reference, it was soon after abbreviated to *Ongiara*. Both words were interpreted as meaning "thunder of waters." Word of the amazing natural wonder was spread orally, and through telling rather than writing, *Ongiara* eventually became *Niagara*.

Who was the first Niagara Falls daredevil?

In October 1829, "the Yankee Leaper," Sam Patch, became the first of the Niagara daredevils by surviving a jump off the main 33.5-metre Canadian Falls. The twenty-two-year-old Patch then went to Rochester, New York, the following month and jumped from the thirty-metre Upper Falls. Disappointed by the small crowd, he chose to repeat the stunt a week later, on Friday, November 13. After a pre-jump celebration at several local taverns and in front of ten thousand spectators, Patch climbed a tower he had built at the brink of the falls. But as he jumped he slipped, causing his feet to miss his planned vertical entry. The crowd heard a very loud noise as he hit the water. His body was found four months later, frozen in the ice of the Genesee River. His grave is marked by a simple wooden board with the inscription: "Sam Patch — Such Is Fame."

Who was the first person to go over Niagara Falls in a barrel?

The first person to brave the falls in a barrel was a woman. Bored with teaching school, and desperate for money, Annie Edson Taylor, a sixty-three-year-old widow (she claimed to be in her forties) chose her birthday, October 24, 1901, to challenge the Canadian Falls. She did it in a wooden pickle barrel made from oak and iron, and padded the inside with a mattress. And she took her cat with her! When she emerged from her plunge, battered and bruised, but with only a minor cut on her forehead, she exclaimed, "No one ought ever to do that again!" Unfortunately, her dream of fame and fortune from the endeavour never materialized. A speaking tour didn't work out, and in 1921, the now eighty-three-year-old Annie Nelson (she had since remarried) died a pauper at the Niagara County Infirmary in Lockport, New York. She is buried in the Stunters Section of Oakwood Cemetery in Niagara Falls, New York.

Of the thirteen attempts to go over the falls in a barrel or enclosed container, three daredevils have died and ten have survived.

DID YOU KNOW ...
that Wolverine, the Marvel Comics character, is often referred to as "the Ol' Canucklehead" due to his Canadian heritage?

Where did the term *Canuck* come from?

Well, no one is quite sure. Although *Canuck* is today a common slang term for a Canadian, the origins of the word are unclear. The first recorded use of the word was around 1835, by Americans in reference to Dutch or French Canadians. At that time it was spelled with a *K* (*Kanuck*). Since around 1850 it has been commonly spelled with a *C*.

DID YOU KNOW ...

that the character of Johnny Canuck was created as a personification of Canada who appeared in early political cartoons of the 1860s and was often depicted standing up to Uncle Sam? The character was revived during the Second World War, this time shown opposing Hitler and the Nazis. In the mid 1970s superhero Captain Canuck was introduced. He wears red tights and "electro-thermic underwear" to keep him warm, and he has a red maple leaf on his forehead. He is endowed with super-strength, super-speed, and his super suit has a variety of technical abilities.

POLICY-MAKERS
AND
GROUND-BREAKERS

Why was Sir Wilfrid Laurier considered one of Canada's greatest prime ministers?

Laurier, a Liberal, was Canada's first francophone prime minister. He holds the record for the most consecutive federal elections won (four), and his fifteen years as prime minister is the longest unbroken term in that office. His nearly forty-five years of public service in the House of Commons is also a record, and no other Canadian politician has served as long (thirty-one years, eight months) as leader of a major political party. Canada expanded under Laurier's tenure, and he was known for his policies of conciliation and compromise between English and French Canada. He was a strong advocate of a French-English partnership in Canada.

Why was Lester Pearson awarded the Nobel Prize?

In 1956 Lester Pearson was minister of foreign affairs in the government of Prime Minister Louis St. Laurent. When the Suez Crisis threatened to embroil France, the United Kingdom, Egypt, and Israel in war, Pearson defused the potential international disaster and created the United Nations Emergency Force to police the disputed area. For this Pearson was awarded the 1957 Nobel Peace Prize. Pearson is considered the father of the modern concept of peacekeeping. Pearson was prime minister of Canada from April 22, 1963, to April 20, 1968.

How did Lincoln Alexander make Canadian history?

In 1968 Lincoln Alexander, representing the Ontario riding of Hamilton West, became Canada's first black member of Parliament. In 1985 Alexander was appointed lieutenant governor of Ontario, making him the first black person in Canada to serve in a vice-regal position. Lincoln Alexander has been awarded the Order of Ontario and has been named a Companion of the Order of Canada.

DID YOU KNOW ...
that the Lincoln M. Alexander Parkway in Hamilton was named in Alexander's honour? Ironically, he never had a driver's licence.

Who was the first black woman to run for the leadership of a Canadian national political party?

Rosemary Brown was born in Jamaica in 1930. When she came to Canada in 1951 to attend university, she encountered racism — other students did not want her for a roommate, and she had difficulty finding employment. She was determined to change things, however, and in 1972 she became the first black woman elected to the British Columbia legislature. Two years later the New Democratic Party asked her to run for the party's leadership. She finished a close second to Ed Broadbent and helped raise public awareness of the potential for both women and minorities in politics.

She continued to work for human rights, women's issues, and world peace throughout her career. She was presented with a total of fifteen honorary doctorates from Canadian universities, the Order of British Columbia (1995), the Order of Canada (Officer, 1996), and in 1973 the United Nations' Human Rights Fellowship. A commemorative stamp was issued by Canada Post in 2009 with a picture of Brown standing in front of the B.C. Legislature building. Rosemary Brown died in 2003.

DID YOU KNOW ...
that Rosemary Brown once said, "To be black and female in a society which is both racist and sexist is to be in the unique position of having nowhere to go but up"?

Who was the first black woman elected to Canada's Parliament?

In 1993 Jean Augustine, representing the Ontario riding of Etobicoke-Lakeshore, became the first black woman elected to the Canadian House of Commons and the first to serve in the federal Cabinet. She served as parliamentary secretary to Prime Minister Jean Chrétien from 1993 to 1996. In 2004 she became the first black woman to occupy the speaker's chair in the House of Commons.

Jean Augustine has received the YWCA Woman of Distinction Award, the Kaye Livingston Award, the Ontario Volunteer Award, *Pride*'s Canadian Black Achievement Award, the Toronto Lions Club Onyx Award, and the Rubena Willis Special Recognition Award. In 2009 she was made a Member of the Order of Canada. She retired from politics in 2015, and a year later Jean Augustine Secondary School opened in Brampton, Ontario.

Who was the first aboriginal Canadian elected to a provincial legislature in Canada?

Frank Calder, of the British Columbia New Democratic Party (NDP), was the first aboriginal person elected anywhere in Canada, and served from 1949 to 1975.

OTHER FIRSTS FOR FIRST NATIONS POLITICIANS

First aboriginal Canadian appointed to Canadian Senate	James Gladstone of Alberta, 1958
First aboriginal Canadian elected to the Canadian House of Commons (first aboriginal Canadian MP)	Leonard Marchand, Kamloops-Cariboo (British Columbia), 1968-74
First aboriginal Canadian woman elected to the Parliament of Canada	Ethel Blondin-Andrew (Western Arctic), 1988-2006

Who was Canada's first female member of Parliament?

In 1921 a small political party called the United Farmers of Ontario chose Agnes Macphail as its candidate for the constituency of South-East Grey (later Grey Bruce). She was the only one of four women running in that year's federal election to win a seat in Parliament, making her Canada's first female MP.

Born on a farm in Grey County in 1890, Macphail had been a schoolteacher, but had never been involved in the suffrage movement. However, she was strong-minded and a champion for the cause of social reform. In an age when most Canadians, including many women, considered politics a man's world, Macphail was a pioneer. She fought for such reforms as crop failure insurance for farmers, unemployment insurance, family allowance, old age pensions, and prison reform. She was a pacifist who spoke against war even when it was unpopular to do so. Macphail held her federal seat until 1940, when a blizzard on election day prevented many of her rural constituents from voting. She turned to provincial politics, and in 1943 she became one of the first two women to serve in the Ontario legislature.

D I D   Y O U   K N O W ...
that a bronze bust of Agnes Macphail was installed in the House of Commons after her death in 1954? Former prime minister John Diefenbaker once said that Canada had produced five great politicians, and Agnes Macphail was one of them.

LEADING THE WAY:
OTHER FEMALE FIRSTS IN CANADIAN POLITICS

First female prime minister		Kim Campbell, Progressive Conservative (1993)
First women in Cabinet	Provincial	Mary Ellen Smith, 1921 (British Columbia)
	Federal	Ellen Fairclough, 1957
First female speaker of the Canadian House of Commons		Jeanne Sauvé (1980–84); also the first woman to serve as governor general (1984-90)

Who was Mary Ann Shadd?

Mary Ann Shadd was a free-born black American teacher, journalist, and abolitionist who moved to Canada West (Ontario) in 1851 following the American government's passage of the Fugitive Slave Act, which was a threat to every black person in the United States, whether free or in servitude. She established schools for escaped slaves and their children who made it to Canada via the Underground Railroad. Against all odds she founded a publication, *The Provincial Freeman*, which was considered the best abolitionist newspaper of the time. She, thus, became the first black female editor and publisher of a newspaper in North America. Her articles attacked not only slavery, but also the stereotyping of black people as being unsophisticated and childlike and always in need of help from white people. At the same time, she disagreed with black leaders in Canada who argued that blacks should live in segregated communities. Shadd believed in integration. After the Civil War she returned to the United States and became the first woman to graduate from Howard University School of Law. She died in Washington, D.C., in 1893.

DID YOU KNOW ...

that Mary Ann Shadd had to deal with gender prejudice, as well as racial bigotry? When subscribers to *The Provincial Freeman* learned that the newspaper's editor was a woman, many of them threatened to cancel their subscriptions. To save the paper she got permission from Reverend William P. Newman, an influential black clergyman, to use his name as a "front." She didn't like having to resort to deception, but felt *The Provincial Freeman*'s message was more important than her pride.

Who were the Famous Five?

The Famous Five, also called the Valiant Five, were: Nellie McClung from Chatsworth, Ontario; Emily Murphy from Cookstown, Ontario; Henrietta Muir Edwards from Montreal; Irene Parlby from London, England; and Louise McKinney from Frankville, Ontario. Each of these women was a pioneer in the cause of the political rights of Canadian women. In 1927 they collectively challenged the Supreme Court of Canada to answer the question, "Does the word *Persons* in section 24 of the British North America Act of 1867 include females?" The Supreme Court's negative response was overturned by the Privy Council in Britain. The Famous Five's successful fight to have women legally recognized as persons threw down gender barriers that had barred women from, among other things, serving as magistrates or being appointed to the Senate of Canada.

INDIVIDUAL ACCOMPLISHMENTS OF THE FAMOUS FIVE

- Nellie McClung — acclaimed novelist, member of the Legislative Assembly of Alberta, first woman member of the Canadian Broadcasting Corporation's Board of Governors.
- Emily Murphy — renowned journalist, first woman magistrate in Canada.
- Henrietta Muir Edwards — co-founder of the National Council of Women of Canada and the Victorian Order of Nurses.
- Irene Parlby — first woman Cabinet minister in Alberta, president of the United Farm Women of Alberta.
- Louise McKinney — first woman to sit in the Legislative Assembly of Alberta, and the first woman elected to a legislature in Canada and the British Empire.

Who was the first woman appointed to the Supreme Court of Canada?

In 1982 Prime Minister Pierre Elliott Trudeau appointed Bertha Wilson to the Supreme Court of Canada. She already had the distinction of being the first woman appointed to the Court of Appeal for Ontario. Bertha Wilson presided over several sensational cases, but perhaps her most controversial ruling came in 1988 in the case of *R. v. Dr. Henry Morgentaler* regarding abortion. Wilson ruled that the existing Canadian law prohibiting abortion was unconstitutional in that it interfered with a woman's rights over her own body.

REBELLIONS

Who was the leader of the 1837–38 Rebellion in Upper Canada?

The leader of the Upper Canada Rebellion was William Lyon Mackenzie, a fiery Scot who was a Reform politician and a journalist. Mackenzie founded a newspaper, the *Colonial Advocate*, in which he attacked the ruling elite, known as the Family Compact. The Family Compact was a tightly knit group of wealthy, influential men who dominated colonial affairs and ruthlessly crushed any threat to their power.

DID YOU KNOW ...
that William Lyon Mackenzie was the first mayor of Toronto (March 27, 1834 – January 14, 1835)?

How did the Family Compact respond to Mackenzie's attacks in the *Colonial Advocate*?

A group of young men disguised as "Indians" broke into Mackenzie's office in York (now Toronto) in broad daylight. They smashed his printing press and threw trays of type into the harbour. Magistrates friendly to the Family Compact initially refused to prosecute the perpetrators, but Mackenzie eventually successfully sued for damages.

Why did Mackenzie turn to armed insurrection?

Mackenzie was elected to the assembly of Upper Canada, but on several occasions he was ejected for speaking against the Family Compact and institutions like the Bank of Upper Canada. He travelled to Britain in hope of drawing attention to the need for political reform in Upper Canada, but was ignored. Mackenzie lost faith in the British parliamentary system and began to speak in favour of the American republican system. In an election in 1836, Sir Francis Bond Head, the lieutenant governor of Upper Canada, actively campaigned for the Family Compact, denouncing Reformers like Mackenzie as traitors. Mackenzie lost his seat in the Assembly, and he looked to other means to bring about change.

Where did the main engagement of the Mackenzie Rebellion take place?

On December 7, 1837, Mackenzie's ragtag army of about five hundred poorly armed rebels met a force of about one thousand militia led by the War of 1812 hero James Fitzgibbon at Montgomery's Tavern, about 5.5 kilometres north of Toronto. There was an exchange of gunfire, then the rebels turned and fled. One rebel was killed and several were wounded. The militia had five or six men wounded. The "battle" of Montgomery's Tavern lasted only a few minutes.

What was the aftermath of the Mackenzie Rebellion?

Two of Mackenzie's followers, Samuel Lount and Peter Matthews, were hanged for their participation in the uprising. About a hundred more were shipped off to a penal colony in Australia. Mackenzie fled to the United States and set up a "republic" on Navy Island in the Niagara River. He was arrested by the Americans and served a year in jail for breach of neutrality laws. For four years he was a political journalist for a New York newspaper. Mackenzie later expressed great disappointment in the American system of government. He said that if he had actually seen it at work sooner, he would never have led a rebellion. Mackenzie was eventually pardoned and returned to Toronto. By this time the Canadian colonies had responsible government, and the power of the Family Compact was broken. Mackenzie served in the legislature until 1858. He died in 1861. Mackenzie's house at 82 Bond Street in Toronto is now a museum.

DID YOU KNOW ...
that Prime Minister William Lyon Mackenzie King was a grandson of William Lyon Mackenzie?

Why is Louis Riel considered the founder of Manitoba?

Born in the Red River Settlement in 1844, Louis Riel was educated in Montreal and rose to leadership among the Métis even though he had only one-eighth aboriginal blood. Riel was eloquent, deeply religious, charismatic, and ambitious. When Canadian government surveyors arrived on Métis land in 1869, Riel sent them packing. In what has been called the Red River Rebellion, Riel and his followers took possession of Fort Garry (Winnipeg). Riel formed a provisional government and drew up a "List of Rights," which was submitted to Ottawa. After much debate and political bargaining, this resulted in the passing of the Manitoba Act and the creation of a new province, which Riel himself named.

Why did Riel have to flee from Manitoba?

When Riel seized Fort Garry, the Canadian government sent out a military force under Colonel Garnet Wolseley to assert federal authority. Riel had to flee to avoid arrest on a charge of murder. There were even rumours that Ontario militiamen with Wolseley intended to lynch him.

Who was Riel charged with killing?

Among the new settlers in the Red River country were a number of people from Ontario who were also members of the Protestant Orange Lodge. The Orangemen, who wielded considerable political clout in Ontario, were strongly anti-French and anti-Catholic, and they were openly contemptuous of Riel and the Métis. One of the most troublesome was a ruffian named Thomas Scott, who repeatedly defied Riel's provisional government. Riel had Scott arrested on charges of interfering with the government. Scott was tried and sentenced to death. Ignoring advisers who wanted the death sentence commuted, Riel had Scott shot by a firing squad. In life Scott had been a bully and a boor, but in death he achieved the status of martyr in Orange Ontario. His execution was the greatest blunder in Riel's career.

What happened to Riel after the Red River Rebellion?

Riel was elected to Parliament, but was unable to take his seat. Prime Minister Alexander Mackenzie granted Riel amnesty, on the condition that Riel accept banishment from Canada for five years. He went to the United States, became an American citizen, and eventually became a schoolteacher in Montana.

Why did Riel return to Canada?

In summer 1884 a deputation of Métis from what is now Saskatchewan went to Montana to seek Riel's help. Once again they were experiencing difficulties with a Canadian government that cared little about their rights and needs. The Métis thought that Riel was the only man who could effectively represent them. The leader of the deputation who went to Montana was Gabriel Dumont.

Who was Gabriel Dumont?

Born in the Red River country in 1837, Gabriel Dumont had the physical skills and the personal traits that made him a natural leader of the Métis people. He was a renowned buffalo hunter, as skilled with a bow and arrow as he was with a rifle. He was an excellent horseman and tracker. While still a boy Dumont proved his courage and fighting ability in a battle with the Sioux. Besides French, he spoke six aboriginal languages fluently. Dumont was a compassionate man who shared his meat from the buffalo hunt with people in need. As a young man he realized that the Métis and the aboriginal people had a common foe in the whites who were moving onto the prairies, and he was instrumental in making peace with long-time enemies of the Métis like the Sioux and the Blackfoot. As the great herds of buffalo dwindled, Dumont helped convince the Métis to turn to farming.

How did Riel's return to Canada lead to rebellion?

Riel wrote to Ottawa, outlining the needs and grievances of the Métis people. The government ignored the letter. Riel, who by this time was clearly mentally unstable, decided that he had a mission from God to be the messiah for the Métis. He declared the Métis community of Batoche to be the capital of a new nation, ruled by him, and the centre of a new church, with Riel as its head. Riel sent messengers to aboriginal leaders like Big Bear and Poundmaker, urging them to join him in a revolt against the Canadian government. Ottawa responded by sending an army to the west.

Where did the main battle of the Northwest Rebellion take place?

There were numerous skirmishes, but the biggest clash between Gabriel Dumont's tough Métis fighters and Major-General Frederick Middleton's army took place at Batoche in May 1885. There were eight hundred Canadian troops against no more than two hundred Métis, but Dumont's men gave the Canadians all they could handle. Not until the Métis were practically out of ammunition were the red-coated soldiers able to effectively press home an attack and rout them.

What happened to Dumont and Riel?

Dumont fled to the United States, where he lived until he was granted amnesty. Riel surrendered and was charged with high treason. He was tried by an all-English, all-Protestant jury and found guilty. Though there were those who believed Riel was insane, government-appointed doctors said he was a reasonable and accountable person who knew the difference between right and wrong. Riel was hanged in Regina on November 16, 1885. The St. Boniface Museum in Manitoba has the moccasins and face mask Riel wore at his execution.

CANADA
AT WAR

Why does Vimy Ridge have a special place in Canadian military history?

Vimy Ridge is an escarpment in France that the Germans occupied early in the First World War. It was a strategic high ground that the Allies desperately wanted to take back. French and British attacks had been utter failures. In a battle lasting from April 9 to April 12, 1917, the Canadian Corps under Lieutenant-General Sir Julian Byng succeeded where the British and French had failed and captured Vimy Ridge. The operation had been meticulously planned, and the soldiers thoroughly trained for the jobs they were to do — something almost unheard of in the Allied armies up to that time. Nonetheless, the fighting was savage. The Canadians had 3,600 killed, seven thousand wounded, and four hundred missing in action. It has been said that the young Canadian nation "came of age" on Vimy Ridge. The capture of Vimy Ridge was the first important Allied victory after more than two years of stalemate on the Western Front.

What happened at Passchendaele?

The Battle of Passchendaele, in which the Allies' goal was to capture the village of that name, was actually a series of battles that began in June 1917 and ended that November. In the final phase it was the Canadians who finally captured the high ground on which the ruins of Passchendaele sat.

Passchendaele was the epitome of everything that was terrible about the First World War: a sea of mud, foul trenches, incompetent generalship, and soldiers dying by the thousands for a few metres of worthless ground. The Allies lost half a million men at Passchendaele, 15,654 of the casualties being Canadian. The Germans lost 350,000 men.

TEN CANADIANS AWARDED THE
VICTORIA CROSS AFTER PASSCHENDAELE

- Lieutenant-Colonel Philip Bent, Halifax, Nova Scotia (awarded posthumously)
- Private Tom Holmes, Owen Sound, Ontario
- Captain Christopher O'Kelly, Winnipeg
- Lieutenant Robert Shankland, Winnipeg
- Private Cecil Kinross, Lougheed, Alberta
- Sergeant George Mullin, Moosomin, Saskatchewan
- Lieutenant Hugh McKenzie, originally from Liverpool, England, immigrated to Canada (awarded posthumously)
- Major George Randolph Pearks, Red Deer, Alberta
- Private James P. Robertson, Medicine Hat, Alberta (awarded posthumously)
- Corporal Collin Barron, Toronto

Who was the top Canadian air ace in the First World War?

William Avery "Billy" Bishop of Owen Sound, Ontario, is on record for scoring seventy-two air victories. That's not counting the three observation balloons he destroyed. Bishop once engaged in an aerial dogfight with the legendary Red Baron, Manfred von Richthofen, though neither was able to shoot the other down. On June 2, 1917, Bishop single-handedly attacked a German airfield and downed three enemy planes, for which he was awarded the Victoria Cross. The Germans actually had a bounty on Billy Bishop's head. They called him "Hell's Handmaiden."

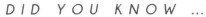

DID YOU KNOW ...
that in the 1942 movie *Captains of the Clouds*, starring James Cagney, Billy Bishop played himself as a
Royal Canadian Air Force officer presiding over the
graduation of cadet pilots?

What type of plane
did Billy Bishop fly?

Bishop scored most of his victories in a Nieuport 17 biplane. He painted
the front of it blue, so he'd be camouflaged against the sky.

DID YOU KNOW ...
that before First World War planes were fitted with
machine guns, enemy pilots flying reconnaissance
would blast away at one another with handguns and
shotguns? One pilot, Malcolm McBean Bell-Irving,
once tried to shoot an enemy pilot with a revolver.
The gun misfired, so Bell-Irving threw it at the German,
hitting him on the side of the head.

What Canadian fighter pilot was credited with killing the Red Baron?

On the morning of April 21, 1918, Royal Air Force 209 Squadron got into a dogfight with the legendary Flying Circus of Manfred von Richthofen, the much-feared Red Baron. Novice Canadian pilot Wilfrid "Wop" May pulled out of the scrap because his machine guns were jammed. The Red Baron spotted him and swooped down for the kill. Flight Commander Arthur "Roy" Brown, of Carleton Place, Ontario, saw May was in trouble and dove after the Red Baron, firing a burst from his guns. This forced the Red Baron to break off his attack on May. He then seemed to pursue May again before gliding his plane to a landing in a field behind Allied lines. Australian soldiers found von Richthofen sitting in the cockpit, dead from a single bullet. The Royal Air Force credited Captain Brown with killing the Red Baron and awarded him the Distinguished Service Cross. However, an Australian anti-aircraft gun crew had also been shooting at von Richthofen's plane, and they claimed it was their bullet that killed the German ace. The controversy continues to this day.

Who was the most decorated Canadian in the First World War?

A fighter pilot, Lieutenant-Colonel William Barker of Dauphin, Manitoba, was Canada's most decorated war hero. He was awarded the Victoria Cross, the Military Cross and two bars, the Distinguished Service Order and bar, France's Croix de Guerre, and Italy's Valore Militare.

What distinction did the Royal Newfoundland Regiment have in the First World War?

The Royal Newfoundland Regiment was the only North American regiment to fight in the disastrous Gallipoli Campaign of 1915. Later, on July 1, 1916, during the Battle of the Somme, the Royal Newfoundland Regiment was almost annihilated at a place called Beaumont Hamel. Lieutenant-Colonel Arthur Lovell Hadow made the observation that the Newfoundlanders' attack failed because "dead men can advance no further." This massive loss of men from a colony with a small population had a profound effect on Newfoundland's history and culture. Today Newfoundland's Memorial Day is observed on July 1.

DID YOU KNOW ...

that Private Thomas Ricketts, age seventeen, of the Royal Newfoundland Regiment, was the youngest person ever to be awarded the Victoria Cross? There is a memorial to Ricketts, who died in 1967, on Water Street in St. John's. A play about him, *The Known Soldier*, was written by Jeff Pitcher.

Why is August 19, 1942, considered one of the darkest days in Canadian military history?

August 19, 1942, was the date of the raid in the French coastal town of Dieppe, which was carried out by an almost all-Canadian force. Code-named

Jubilee, the operation was supposed to be a surprise attack. Far from being surprised, the German defenders were ready and waiting. The Canadians had 916 killed, 586 wounded among those who made it back to England, and 1,946 taken prisoner.

What was "The Devil's Brigade"?

The First Special Service Force was an elite, specially trained commando unit made of Canadian and American soldiers. Originally intended to fight the Japanese in the Aleutian Islands, they were used on special operations in Italy and France in 1943 and 1944. Because the commandos often operated at night with their faces blackened with boot polish, the Germans called them *Die schwarzen Teufel* — the black devils. They would tag demolished German military property and dead German soldiers with labels that said, in German, "The worst is yet to come." The 1968 movie *The Devil's Brigade* starring William Holden and Cliff Robertson was loosely based on the First Special Service Force's story.

Which Canadian was the real "Tunnel King" in the true story of the Great Escape?

Canadian fighter pilot Wally Floody had worked in the mines of Northern Ontario, so when he wound up as a prisoner of war in Stalag Luft III after being shot down over France in 1941, he had the very skills the camp's escape committee was looking for. Floody was the principal architect and digger of the tunnels that were dug as part of a major breakout attempt.

However, Floody did not get a chance to get out on the night of the escape. The German guards became suspicious a few days before the event and transferred Floody to another POW camp. Floody returned to Canada after the war and was later employed as a technical adviser on the set of the 1963 film *The Great Escape*.

How did a cigarette case save the life of *Star Trek*'s "Scotty" during the Normandy Campaign?

Vancouver-born James Doohan stormed Juno Beach with the Canadian army on D-Day, and he allegedly helped knock out a German machine gun. A few days after the landing, as his regiment advanced into Normandy, Doohan was hit by machine-gun fire. He received bullet wounds in his leg and right hand. Another bullet struck him in the chest and could have been fatal, but was deflected by a metal cigarette case in his pocket. As a result of the injury to his right hand, Doohan had to have his middle finger amputated. Years later, when Doohan played chief engineer Montgomery "Scotty" Scott of the Starship *Enterprise*, the TV show's producers took care to hide Scotty's disfigured hand from viewers. In close-up shots of Scotty's hands working the controls of the transporter, "stand-in" hands were used. In the episode "Trouble with Tribbles," when both of Scott's hands are in view while he holds a pile of the creatures, his missing finger is supposedly buried in tribble fur.

How did a Canadian fighter pilot knock Germany's top general out of the war?

Charley Fox of Guelph, Ontario, had already participated in the Battle of Britain, flown in the D-Day invasion of Normandy, attacked V1 and V2 rocket-launching sites, and earned the Distinguished Flying Cross and Bar, when he performed one of the most important single acts of the war. On July 17, 1944, Fox was flying across the French countryside looking for "targets of opportunity" when he spotted a German military staff car racing along a tree-lined road. While his wing mate Steve Randall flew cover for him, Fox dove at the German car and strafed it. The car went off the road and rolled over. Allied intelligence later learned that Germany's top general, Field Marshal Erwin Rommel, had suffered serious head injuries when his car was attacked by a fighter plane. Several pilots sought credit for strafing Rommel, but investigation eventually proved beyond a doubt that Charley Fox was the man who had put the legendary Desert Fox out of action. Fox had recorded the incident in his logbook, but never boasted of it. On October 18, 2008, at the age of eighty-eight, Charley Fox was killed in a car accident near Tillsonburg, Ontario.

?   *DID YOU KNOW ...*
that D-Day was the first time the Canadian army fought under the Red Ensign? Before that Canadians had fought under the British Union Jack.

What is the "Diefenbunker"?

The "Diefenbunker" is the nickname of Canadian Forces Station (CFS) Carp, a former Canadian military facility located in Carp, Ontario, just outside Ottawa.

The year was 1958, and the world was at the height of the Cold War, with the threat of a nuclear missile attack becoming a stark and frightening reality. In reaction, Canada's prime minister at the time, John Diefenbaker, authorized the creation of around fifty Emergency Government Headquarters across Canada. These shelters were part of what came to be known as the Continuity of Government Plan, meant to protect various members of government in the event of a nuclear attack. Members of the opposition government referred to these bunkers as "Diefenbunkers," and the name stuck. CFS Carp was the largest of these shelters, capable of sustaining 565 people for up to a month, and it was also the closest to the nation's capital. The four-storey underground bunker was finally decommissioned in 1994, and in 1998 it reopened as a museum and was designated a National Historic Site of Canada. Today it continues to operate as a museum, offering tours year-round.

How many Canadians served in the Korean War?

Altogether, 26,792 Canadians served in the Korean War. Of the 1,558 casualties, 516 were fatal. The names of the fallen are inscribed in the *Korean War Book of Remembrance*, on display at the Canadian War Museum in Ottawa.

Where is Canada's Highway of Heroes?

On August 24, 2007, the Ontario Ministry of Transportation announced that the stretch of Highway 401 from Glen Miller Road in Trenton, Ontario, to the intersection of the Don Valley Parkway and Highway 404 in Toronto would be called Highway of Heroes in honour of Canadian Forces personnel killed in Afghanistan. This part of the highway is the route for the processions carrying slain soldiers' bodies from CFB Trenton to the coroner's office in Toronto. People line the overpasses to pay their respects as the processions pass by. Signs depicting a shield decorated with a poppy mark the Highway of Heroes.

HEROES
AND
LEGENDS

Who was Big Joe Mufferaw?

The legendary Big Joe Mufferaw of the Ottawa Valley was, in fact, Joseph Montferrand, the Montreal-born hero of Quebec loggers. As a youth Montferrand was a voyageur for the Hudson's Bay Company, but in 1827 he went to work in the woods. He stood six foot four, was powerfully built, and it was said that as a lad of sixteen he had knocked out a Royal Navy boxing champion in a bout in Quebec City. Montferrand was easy-going and generous by nature, but in the brawling timber camps and rugged communities of the Ottawa Valley, he was a force to be reckoned with, especially in the battles between the French Canadians and Irish hoodlums known as Shiners. Montferrand allegedly single-handedly routed a gang of Shiners when they thought they had him trapped on the bridge between Hull and Bytown (now Ottawa). He also walloped the Shiner's main tough guy, Big Martin Hennesy, in a celebrated saloon fight. Montferrand allegedly could leap into the air and leave the heel marks of his logging boots in a saloon ceiling. After his death in 1864, Montferrand was immortalized in song and story. His admirers have included Sir Wilfrid Laurier, author of a biography, and Stompin' Tom Connors, who wrote the ballad "Big Joe Mufferaw."

Who was the Cape Breton Giant?

Angus MacAskill was born in Scotland in 1825 but grew up (literally) in St. Ann's, Cape Breton. MacAskill was a normal-size baby, but he grew to an adult height of seven feet nine inches. He weighed 193 kilograms and had a girth of 203 centimetres, the largest known on a non-obese man. Initially MacAskill was a farmer and a fisherman, but due to his size and incredible physical strength he went on the road with a circus. He returned to Cape Breton with a small fortune and opened a general store which he ran until his sudden death in 1863 at the age of thirty-eight. There are many stories about MacAskill's tremendous feats of strength and of his acts of kindness and generosity. MacAskill was once listed in the *Guinness World Records* as the world's biggest non-pathological giant. He is still regarded as a folk hero in Cape Breton. His grave can still be seen at Englishtown, Cape Breton, near a small museum that displays some of his personal belongings.

Who was Klondike Joe Boyle?

Born in Toronto in 1867, Joseph W. Boyle lived an adventurous life worthy of a Hollywood movie. He was a sailor, an entrepreneur, a boxer, a gold hunter, a secret agent, and the confidant of royalty. He had already packed a lifetime of exotic experience into his thirty years when he joined the Klondike Gold Rush in 1897. Boyle made a fortune by using hydraulic methods to extract gold. In 1904–05 Boyle financed a Yukon hockey team, the Wanderers, which unsuccessfully challenged the Ottawa Silver Seven for the Stanley Cup. In the First World War Boyle recruited and equipped a fifty-man machine-gun company. His unit was incorporated into the Canadian army. In 1917 Boyle went to Russia to help organize the country's chaotic railway system. In the midst of the Russian Revolution, Boyle managed to become a national hero to Romania by rescuing fifty high-ranking Romanians, as well as some important documents from the country. It was even rumoured that Boyle had a romantic affair with Romania's Queen Marie. Boyle was decorated by the governments of Great Britain, France, Romania, and Russia. He died in 1923 and is buried in Woodstock, Ontario.

Why is "Wild Goose Jack" a hero to conservationists?

John Thomas "Jack" Miner was born in Ohio, but he moved with his family to Essex County, Ontario, as a boy. In his youth Miner was an avid hunter and trapper, but had a change of heart after his brother was killed in a hunting accident. Miner began to take an interest in nature, particularly birds and migration. In 1904 he created a pond on his farm with a few clipped, tame Canada geese that he hoped would attract wild geese. It took a few years, but eventually thousands of wild geese were attracted to Miner's homemade sanctuary, the first of its kind in North America. Miner was the first to start banding ducks and geese in order to unlock the mysteries of migration routes. A direct result of his studies was the 1916 Migratory Bird Treaty between Canada and the United States. Right up until his death in 1944, Wild Goose Jack lectured on the importance of conservation. In 1943 King George VI presented him with the Order of the British Empire (OBE).

Why is Sir Wilfred Grenfell fondly remembered in Newfoundland and Labrador?

Wilfred Grenfell was an English medical missionary who founded the Grenfell Mission and opened the first hospital at Battle Harbour in 1893. From his headquarters in St. Anthony, Newfoundland, Grenfell cruised the coasts of Newfoundland and Labrador, bringing medical assistance to people who might otherwise never see a doctor. The International Grenfell Association, which grew from the mission, still funds scholarships for medical training. Grenfell was knighted for his work, and in 1911 he received the Murchison Prize from the Royal Geographic Society. In 1997 he was inducted into the Canadian Medical Hall of Fame. There is a statue of Grenfell in St. Anthony, and his house is now a museum.

What is the motto of the RCMP?

The official motto of the RCMP is *Maintiens le Droit*, meaning "Uphold the Right." It is not, and never has been "We always get our man." That phrase can be traced back to an article that appeared in the Fort Benton, Montana, *Record* in April 1877. "The Mounted Police are worse than bloodhounds when they catch the track of a smuggler, and they fetch their man every time." Fort Benton was the main supply depot for the whisky traders who were smuggling liquor into Canada.

Who was Sam Steele?

Samuel Benfield Steele, born in Medonte Township, Upper Canada, in 1849, was the quintessential Mountie. He was one of the first men to sign up with the force, and he was in the Great March of 1874. Steele was involved in almost all of the significant events of nineteenth-century western Canada, from the Northwest Rebellion to the construction of the Canadian Pacific Railway through the Rocky Mountains. He directed the manhunts for outlaws and killers, including the notorious renegades Almighty Voice and Charcoal. When the federal government threatened to disband the NWMP, Sam Steele was the force's staunchest defender. Tall, handsome, ramrod-straight, and a man of action, Sam Steele was the personification of the romantic ideal of the Mountie.

Who was the Angel of Long Point?

Abigail Becker, a big, strong woman who stood six foot two, was the wife of a trapper and fisherman who lived on Long Point, a peninsula jutting from the Canadian shore into the eastern end of Lake Erie. The waters around Long Point were deadly to shipping because of the many shifting sandbars. Becker gained international fame for her heroic rescues of men from several shipwrecks, most notably that of the schooner *Conductor* in November 1854. Even though she couldn't swim, Becker braved the cold, rough water to save the *Conductor's* captain and seven crewmen. For this courageous deed she received a letter of commendation from Queen Victoria, a letter of congratulations from the governor general of Canada, and was awarded a gold medal by the Life Saving Benevolent Association of New York. She was the guest of honour at a banquet in Buffalo, where she was presented with a purse of $550. In 1860 she was visited by the Prince of Wales (later King Edward VII). Abigail Becker is remembered in the lore of Great Lakes navigation as the Angel of Long Point.

What great height did Sharon Wood reach?

On May 20, 1986, twenty-nine-year-old Sharon Wood of Halifax became the first North American woman to climb to the summit of Mount Everest. She was part of a twelve-person team (no porters) called Everest Light, led by Jim Elzinga of Calgary. The expedition ascended the Chinese side of the mountain. By the time the climbers established a camp two thousand feet below the summit, most of them were exhausted. Sharon Wood made the final ascent with Dwayne Congdon of Canmore, Alberta. The pair remained at the top of the world for only twenty minutes, because an eighty-kilometre-an-hour wind was blowing and it was almost sundown.

How did Clara Brett Martin challenge the Law Society of Upper Canada?

In 1891 seventeen-year-old Clara Brett Martin, an honours graduate of Toronto's Trinity College, applied for admission to study law at the Law Society of Upper Canada. She was refused on the grounds that only "persons" could study law, and women were not recognized as persons. Martin then petitioned to be admitted as a student-at-law, with the support of the

Dominion Women's Enfranchisement Association and a few members of the Ontario Legislature. In 1892 a bill was passed that permitted the law society to admit women to study law. However, it limited women lawyers to being solicitors. They could not be barristers. That meant they could have clients, but could not represent them in court. This was a compromise intended to appease the suffrage movement. Clara Brett Martin continued to press for the right to be a full barrister. Among her supporters were Emily Stowe, Lady Aberdeen, and Ontario premier Sir Oliver Mowat. Martin finally won her fight in 1897, when she became the first woman admitted to the bar in Canada and in the British Empire.

DID YOU KNOW ...

that before Clara Brett Martin's heroic struggle to be allowed to study law, women were barred not only from being lawyers, but they were also forbidden to be magistrates, coroners, jurors, legislators, or voters? Anti-suffrage hardliners in the Law Society of Upper Canada put up a stiff fight to keep Martin out, because they were afraid that if women became lawyers, they would soon be challenging the laws that denied them the right to vote.

PRODIGIES
OF SCIENCE,
INVENTION,
AND MEDICINE

Why are David Fife and Charles Saunders heroes to western Canadian wheat growers?

In the early 1840s a Peterborough, Ontario, farmer named David Fife was the object of ridicule from his neighbours because of experiments he had been conducting to create a strain of wheat suited to the cold Canadian climate. By 1843 he had come up with a new strain called Red Fife that ripened more quickly than other strains and so was adaptable to the short Canadian growing season. It also made high-quality flour. Half a century later Charles Saunders crossed Red Fife with an Indian strain called Hard Red Calcutta and created Marquis wheat. It was much more resistant to disease than Red Fife, produced more grains to the bushel, and was ready to harvest in just one hundred days. Marquis wheat was introduced in 1907. Within twelve years 90 percent of Canadian wheat fields were growing Marquis.

Which Canadian is known as the Father of Standard Time?

Since arriving in Canada from Scotland as a youth, Sir Sandford Fleming could, by 1878, boast of a long list of accomplishments. He was co-founder of the Royal Canadian Institute and a renowned engineer, surveyor, writer, and explorer. However, Fleming is best known as the Father of Standard Time. Before Fleming presented his brilliant idea for global time zones in 1878, people in every community set their clocks by the sun, and therefore there was total chaos as far as things like train schedules were concerned. Fleming's proposal was not without opposition. The International Meridian Conference of 1884 rejected the zones he had laid out. Religious groups denounced the whole idea as contrary to God's law, and they accused Fleming of being a communist. Nonetheless, by 1883 all railways in North America had adopted the system, and by 1929 all the major countries in the world had accepted Fleming's time zones.

Who was Canada's first female doctor?

In 1867 Emily Jennings Stowe of Norwich Township, Upper Canada (now Ontario), graduated from the New York Medical College for Women, which she had attended because no medical school in Canada would accept female students. The prevailing Victorian attitudes were that women were "too delicate" to be doctors and that "proper" women did not concern themselves with things like human anatomy. Stowe opened a medical office in Toronto, thus becoming the first woman doctor in Canada. However, the province passed a law that required all American-trained doctors in Ontario to attend a term of lectures at an Ontario medical school and pass a set of examinations. Stowe and another female medical student, Jennie Trout, attended the lectures and passed the examinations, in spite of the most reprehensible efforts of male teachers and students to humiliate and discourage them. Thanks to her lifelong fight to change attitudes, by the time of Stowe's death in 1903, there were more than 120 female doctors in Canada.

How did Dr. Frederick Banting of Ontario astound American businessmen?

Dr. Banting is credited with being the person most responsible for the discovery of insulin in 1921, though he shared the honours with Charles Best and Dr. John James R. Macleod. American pharmaceutical companies offered Banting huge sums of money for the patent on insulin. They wanted to build an insulin clinic in a large American city, put Banting in charge, and make the lifesaving medication available to diabetics who could afford to pay for it. Banting astounded them when he said that insulin was his gift to the human race, and it would be available for everybody who needed it; it would not be a commodity for anybody's personal profit. Banting and Macleod received the Nobel Prize for Medicine. Banting shared his half of the honorarium with Best. Banting also received a knighthood.

D I D   Y O U   K N O W ...

that Dr. Frederick Banting worked with the Royal
Canadian Air Force in studying the physiological
effects of high-altitude aerial combat on pilots? On
February 21, 1941, Banting was on his way to England
to conduct tests on a new flying suit, when he was
killed in a plane crash off the coast of Newfoundland.

Where in Canada was Pablum invented?

In the late 1920s Toronto's Hospital for Sick Children was renowned for its surgeons, but like most other hospitals it had a high rate of infant mortality. Three physicians at SickKids — Dr. Alan Brown, Dr. Theodore Drake, and Dr. Frederick Tisdall, all from Ontario — believed that poor diet was a major factor in the high rate of illness and death among babies. While they were proponents of breast-feeding, they knew that mother's milk lacked iron. They also knew that the first solid food most babies were fed was white bread, which lacked many nutrients. They worked together, and with the assistance of laboratory technician Ruth Herbert and chemist Harry Engel, to develop a nutrient-rich food that would be easy for mothers to prepare and for babies to digest. The recipe for their pre-cooked cereal included wheat, corn, oats, wheat germ, brewer's yeast, bone meal, alfalfa leaf, iron, and iron salt. They called it "Pablum" from the Greek word for food, *pabulum*. Pablum was fed to babies in SickKids and then became available to the public in 1931. It was a breakthrough in nutritional science because, among other benefits, it contributed to a decrease in the number of cases of rickets, a crippling childhood disease caused by insufficient vitamin D. For twenty-five years the Hospital for Sick Children received a royalty on the sales of Pablum.

What may have been Alexander Graham Bell's motivation for inventing the telephone?

Alexander Graham Bell's wife and mother were both deaf, and they influenced Bell's work to a great extent. Also, his father, brother, and grandfather were interested in elocution and speech.

Scottish-born Bell came to Canada when he was twenty-three. His interest in the study of the human voice led him to learn the Mohawk language and to translate its unwritten vocabulary into Visible Speech symbols. Years later Bell conducted research on speech and hearing, which eventually led to experimentation with hearing devices and with electricity and sound. The most famous of these experiments led to the first patent on the telephone, filed in 1876.

CANADIAN DISASTERS

What was the deadliest man-made disaster in Canada's history?

On December 6, 1917, the French munitions ship SS *Mont Blanc*, which was loaded with explosives, collided with the Norwegian vessel SS *Imo* in a strait leading to Halifax Harbour. The subsequent fire onboard the *Mont Blanc* ignited her volatile cargo, causing a massive explosion that devastated a vast area of Halifax. Approximately two thousand people were killed by the blast, the resulting fires, and collapsing buildings, and an estimated nine thousand others were injured. The blast was the largest man-made explosion before the development of nuclear weapons, releasing the energy of about 2.9 kilotons of TNT.

How did Hurricane Hazel take the lives of five Toronto firemen?

When Hurricane Hazel struck Toronto on the night of October 15, 1954, the 124-kilometre-per-hour winds that came shrieking across Lake Ontario certainly were frightful, but the greatest danger was caused by the more than two hundred millimetres of rain that fell in twenty-four hours on ground already saturated from three weeks of steady precipitation. It wasn't the wind that made Hurricane Hazel a killer, it was the flooding. Rescue workers spent long, dangerous hours pulling people out of raging rivers and creeks, and plucking them from the roofs of houses. In one tragic incident, the rescuers became the victims. Eight members of the Kingsway-Lambton Volunteer Fire Department roared off in their fire engine in response to a call about a motorist stuck in his car. The roads of Toronto had been turned into rivers. The fire engine was caught in a wash so powerful, it rolled over. Five of the men, Clarence Collins, Frank

Mercer, Roy Oliver, David Palmeter, and Angus Small, were drowned. A plaque commemorates their sacrifice.

Who were the heroes of Canada's worst maritime disaster?

Early in the morning of May 29, 1914, the ocean liner *Empress of Ireland* collided with the Norwegian freighter *Storstad* in the St. Lawrence River. The liner's hull was ripped open, and she began to sink quickly in the frigid water. It was the worst marine disaster in Canadian history, costing the lives of 1,012 people. There were, however, acts of heroism. Sir Henry Seton-Karr, a famous big game hunter, forcibly put his life jacket on a man who didn't have one. Seton-Karr drowned. Dr. Jonas Grant, the ship's doctor, lost his clothes when he squeezed out through a porthole, and he was naked when he was pulled into a lifeboat. He asked for a pair of pants and then went straight to work treating injured and shock-stricken survivors. Robert Crellin of British Columbia was in the water when he took eight-year-old Florence Barbour on his back. The little girl lost both her parents in the shipwreck, so Crellin and his wife adopted her. There had been 138 children aboard the ship. Florence was one of only four who survived.

DID YOU KNOW ...
that the deadliest pandemic to hit Canada was the Spanish flu outbreak of 1918–19, which claimed an estimated fifty thousand Canadian lives. It sadly came on the heels of the First World War, a conflict that had already resulted in close to sixty-one thousand Canadian deaths.

How did a projectionist and an usher become heroes during Canada's worst movie theatre fire?

On the afternoon of January 9, 1927, fire broke out on the balcony of Montreal's Laurier Palace movie theatre. The audience was mostly unchaperoned children. At the cry of "Fire!" the ground floor was quickly evacuated. But up on the balcony all was chaos. Terrified children rushed for the two narrow stairways. At the west stairway a young usher named Paul Champagne, who had not immediately fled his post as the other ushers had done, took charge. Champagne made the children exit down the stairs and out to the street in an orderly manner. Having saved the lives of one group of children, Champagne tried to go back for the others, but was blocked by thick smoke. Meanwhile, projectionist Emile Massicote looked out of his small projection room and saw the crush of children trying to push their way through the east stairway door. The projection room had a window that opened onto the theatre's marquee. Massicote shouted that he had a way out, but the shrieking, hysterical children didn't hear him. Massicote grabbed two screaming, kicking children, dragged them to the window, and put them out on the marquee. Then he went back for two more. Massicote rescued thirty children before the heavy smoke forced him to climb out onto the marquee himself. The Laurier Palace theatre fire killed seventy-eight children; a tragedy that would have been even worse but for the heroics of an usher and a projectionist.

Who was "Eddy," and how did he help save dozens from a terrible shipboard fire in Toronto Harbour?

When fire broke out aboard the Great Lakes passenger liner *Noronic* in Toronto Harbour early on the morning of September 17, 1949, only a skeleton crew was aboard, and most of the passengers were asleep in their staterooms. The fire spread through the ship rapidly, and several of the crew on night duty hurried ashore without alerting the passengers. However, a bellboy identified only as Eddy did not shirk his duty. As soon as he was aware of the fire he ran to a cabin on A-deck, where other bellboys were sleeping and awakened them. Eddy and two of the boys then woke up as many passengers as they could by banging on cabin doors. Eddy smashed down one door with an axe to get a hysterical woman out of her stateroom. Then Eddy and his pals knotted bed sheets together to make a ladder that people could use to climb down to the dock. Only when they were sure no one else was left in their section of the ship did Eddy and the other two bellboys save themselves. A total of 118 people died as a result of the *Noronic* fire.

DID YOU KNOW ...
that the most deadly natural disaster in Canada's recorded history occurred in 1775, when a devastating hurricane hit Newfoundland, claiming four thousand victims, most of them fishermen aboard the nearly one thousand ships that sunk during the storm?

INTREPID
EXPLORERS

How do we know the Vikings were the first Europeans to explore the East Coast of Canada?

Norse sagas tell us that about the year 1000, Viking leaders like Leif Ericsson and Thorfinn Karlsefini sailed from Iceland and Greenland, and they landed at places they called Helluland, Markland, and Vinland. Historians disagree on the exact locations for these place names, but suggest Helluland could have been Baffin Island or Labrador, Markland could have been Newfoundland, and Vinland could have been Nova Scotia. Archeological finds at L'Anse aux Meadows in Newfoundland prove beyond a doubt that the Vikings had a settlement there. A second Viking site may have been discovered by archaeologists in Newfoundland in 2015, though this site is much farther south. Research is ongoing by an international team of archeologists who continue to work at the site at Point Rosee to discover its mysteries.

Who was John Cabot?

He was actually Giovanni Caboto, a Genoese mariner who in 1496 convinced King Henry VII of England that he could do for the English what another Italian, Christopher Columbus, had failed to do for the Spanish — reach China by sailing west. On his historic voyage in 1497, Cabot made a landfall in North America. The site is still disputed. It could have been the coast of Maine, mainland Nova Scotia, Cape Breton Island, Newfoundland, or Labrador. Cabot called his discovery the "new-found-land." A year later Cabot set out on another voyage and vanished from history.

What were Jacques Cartier's accomplishments?

Jacques Cartier's greatest accomplishment was the discovery of the St. Lawrence River in 1535. He explored it as far as the site of Montreal in hope that it would lead to the Pacific Ocean. Cartier also made the first territorial claims that were the beginning of a French empire in North America. He discovered Prince Edward Island, proved that Newfoundland is an island (previous explorers had thought it was part of the mainland), and learned of an aboriginal cure for scurvy made from the leaves and bark of white cedar — a cure that was subsequently lost.

DID YOU KNOW ...
that it was Jacques Cartier who gave Canada its name? He heard an Iroquois call his community *kan-ata*, the Iroquoian word for village. Cartier thought it was the name of the entire country.

DID YOU KNOW ...
that Jacques Cartier found what he thought were diamonds and took a bushel of them back to France? They turned out to be worthless quartz. This resulted in a new catch-phrase in France: *faux comme les diamants du Canada* — "as false as Canadian diamonds."

Why is Samuel de Champlain called "The Father of New France" and "The Father of Acadia"?

Samuel de Champlain battled against the odds to establish a permanent French colony in the New World even though previous attempts had failed. In 1608 he founded Quebec City. Without that colony there would have been no Canada as we know it. Champlain was the first explorer to probe the wilderness of Quebec and Ontario, and he laid the foundations for the all-important fur trade. Though he was forced to surrender a besieged and starving Quebec to English privateers in 1629, he returned in 1633 to rebuild the French colony. It was a thriving community by the time Champlain died in 1635.

How did Champlain make the Iroquois the arch-enemies of New France?

In 1609 Champlain and two or three other Frenchmen used their firearms to help their Huron, Algonquin, and Montagnais friends defeat their Iroquois enemies. In 1615 Champlain and a dozen or so French soldiers joined a Huron invasion of the Iroquois homeland on the south shore of Lake Ontario. Their attack on an Iroquois town failed, and the invaders withdrew. Champlain was wounded in the fighting and had to be carried in a basket. The Iroquois never forgave the French.

Who was "the Columbus of the Great Lakes"?

Étienne Brûlé was a protégé of Samuel de Champlain, and the first European who could actually be called a frontiersman. Champlain sent young Brûlé to live among the aboriginal people to learn their languages and their customs. Brûlé readily took to life in the wilderness. He travelled widely with the First Nations, and there is evidence that he was the first European to see all of the Great Lakes except Lake Michigan. This has led some historians to call him "the Columbus of the Great Lakes."

What was the most infamous mutiny in Canadian history?

The most infamous act of mutiny in Canadian history was that of the crew of the *Discovery* against Captain Henry Hudson in 1611. It made a tragic hero out of Hudson, and added an intriguing mystery to Canada's Arctic lore.

Why did Henry Hudson's crew mutiny?

When Henry Hudson sailed his ship *Discovery* through the Hudson Strait (known then as the Furious Overfall) and into Hudson Bay in 1610, he thought he had reached the Pacific Ocean. The ship was trapped at the bottom of James Bay by ice, and the crew spent a hellish winter there. In the spring, when the ice finally went out of the bay, the starving survivors wanted to go back to England. Hudson told the men they were going to continue searching for the route to China. A group of conspirators seized control of the ship. They put Hudson, his teenaged son, a few sick men, and any crewmen who were loyal to the captain into a boat and set it adrift. The fate of Hudson and his fellow castaways remains a mystery to this day.

DID YOU KNOW ...

that of the twenty-two men who originally sailed with Henry Hudson, only eight made it back to England alive? Four of them were tried on charges of mutiny, but were acquitted. They conveniently managed to lay blame for the crime on men who were already dead. Moreover, because these survivors of the Hudson expedition were now experienced Arctic mariners, they were very valuable to the British Admiralty.

Who was known as "The Man Who Mapped the West"?

David Thompson of London, England, came to Canada while just a boy as an apprentice with the Hudson's Bay Company. A fellow employee taught him the basics of surveying, and this became the love of Thompson's life. In 1797 he went over to the rival North West Company, which expressed more interest in exploration than the Hudson's Bay Company had. Over the next fifteen years, usually under extremely primitive conditions, Thompson surveyed and mapped more territory than any individual explorer had done before him. It was a feat that would not be matched by anyone who came after. There were several occasions when Thompson was fortunate to emerge from the wilderness alive. At the age of forth-three Thompson went to Montreal to work on his masterpiece, his "Map of the North-West Territory of the Province of Canada." Thompson's "Great Map," as it came to be called, measures three metres by 1.98 metres. It shows, in detail, the region between Hudson Bay and the Pacific Ocean, from the Great Lakes and the Columbia River in the south to Lake Athabasca in the north. Thompson had travelled more than eighty thousand kilometres across that land in order to fill in the empty spaces. By the time of his death in 1857, Thompson was all but forgotten. Today he is recognized as one of the greatest mapmakers who ever lived.

?

DID YOU KNOW ...
that from 1816 to 1826 David Thompson was "Astronomer and Surveyor" for the British Boundary Commission? He helped to establish the Ontario section of the United States–Canada border.

What important scientific discovery was made by Arctic explorer James Clark Ross?

- -

In 1828 British explorer James Clark Ross and his uncle John Ross, both veterans of the Arctic, sailed their ship *Victory* to the Boothia Peninsula, the northernmost extension of mainland Canada. Their ship became trapped in the ice, and the two Rosses and their men were stranded for many months. While they awaited a thaw that they hoped would release the ship, James Ross made several journeys by sled. On one of these expeditions he reached a spot where he noticed the needle of a device called a dip circle (a type of compass) was pointing straight down. He realized he was standing above the North Magnetic Pole, the location of which had previously been unknown.

When did the first ship successfully navigate the Northwest Passage?

In 1905 Norwegian explorer Roald Amundsen sailed his ship *Gjoa* from
east to west through the Northwest Passage. In 1942 the RCMP vessel *St.
Roch* became the first ship to successfully navigate the Northwest Passage
from west to east.

What famous explorer played hockey in the Arctic?

A recent discovery in a letter from British Arctic explorer Sir John Franklin
to Roderick Murchison, dated November 6, 1825, records: "Till the snow
fell the game of hockey played on the ice was the morning's sport."

Franklin's men were wintering during his second Arctic expedition at
Fort Franklin (now called Deline) in Canada's North-West Territories on
the shore of Great Bear Lake in October 1825. However, it isn't clear if the
people participating in this activity were wearing skates. More likely, they
were playing field hockey. Still, that doesn't stop Deline today from laying
claim to hosting the very first "hockey" game in North America.

What is the mystery of the Franklin Expedition?

Sir John Franklin was an English Royal Navy officer and Arctic explorer. He and his crew disappeared on his last expedition, in 1845–46, while they were attempting to chart and navigate a section of the Northwest Passage in the Canadian Arctic. The icebound ships were abandoned, and the entire crew perished from starvation, hypothermia, tuberculosis, lead poisoning, and scurvy. For years the whereabouts of the expedition's two ships, *Erebus* and *Terror*, were unknown. Many searches and expeditions were launched over the years to try and locate the vessels, but it wasn't until the twenty-first century that a breakthrough finally came. In September 2014 it was announced that the wreck of HMS *Erebus* had been rediscovered. And just two years later, in September 2016, the Arctic Research Foundation expedition announced that it had found the wreck of HMS *Terror*. Both sites have been designated as National Historic Sites.

DID YOU KNOW ...
that more ships and men were lost looking for Sir John Franklin than in the expedition itself?

How did Franklin get the moniker "the man who ate his boots"?

During his earlier Coppermine Expedition (1819–22), Sir John Franklin lost eleven of the twenty men in his party. Most of the men died of starvation, but it is believed there was also at least one murder, and there were suggestions that the survivors even resorted to cannibalism. When they ran out of food, the men were forced to eat lichen and even attempted to eat their own leather boots. This gained Franklin the nickname of "the man who ate his boots."

Who was the first Canadian astronaut?

Marc Garneau, born in Quebec City in 1949, was the first Canadian in space. He had the rank of commander in the Canadian Navy, when in 1984 he was one of six applicants chosen from over four thousand for the Canadian Astronaut Program. After his initial flight aboard the space shuttle *Challenger* as a payload specialist in 1984, Garneau flew further missions in 1996 and 2000, making him the first Canadian to go into space three times. Captain Garneau logged almost 678 hours in space before he retired as an astronaut. He has been made a Companion of the Order of Canada, and a Toronto high school has been named in his honour. A squadron of the Royal Canadian Air Cadets is also named after Marc Garneau. In the 2008 federal election Garneau ran as the Liberal candidate for the riding of Westmount–Ville-Marie, and won by more than nine thousand votes.

Who was the first Canadian woman in space?

Roberta Bondar, born in Sault Ste. Marie, Ontario, in 1945, became the first female Canadian astronaut in January 1992, when she flew aboard the space shuttle *Discovery* to perform life science and material science experiments in the Spacelab. She was only the second Canadian in space and the first neurologist. Dr. Bondar left the Canadian Space Agency in September 1992 to pursue research. She has degrees in zoology and agriculture from the University of Guelph, experimental pathology from Western University, neurobiology from the University of Toronto, and has been admitted as a Fellow of the Royal College of Physicians and Surgeons of Canada as a specialist in neurobiology. Dr. Bondar has received numerous honorary degrees and appointments, and she has been inducted into the Canadian Medical Hall of Fame. She has also received the Order of Canada, and she has five schools across the country named after her. In addition to all this, Roberta Bondar is a renowned landscape photographer.

ENTERTAIN ME

Which Canadian actress was known as "America's Sweetheart"?

Gladys Louise Smith was born in Toronto on April 8, 1892. When Gladys was fifteen she landed a role in a Broadway play. But the director thought young Gladys needed to change her name. So she became Mary Pickford. Pickford went on to become a pioneer in the early days of Hollywood. She was one of the earliest stars to be billed under her name, and she was one of the most popular actresses of the 1910s and 1920s, earning her the nicknames "Queen of the Movies" and "America's Sweetheart." Pickford won the second ever Academy Award for Best Actress for her first sound film role in *Coquette* in 1929, and she went on to co-found the United Artists film studio. She and her second husband, actor Douglas Fairbanks, were considered Hollywood royalty, and they called their Beverly Hills mansion Pickfair.

DID YOU KNOW ...
that Mary Pickford was born on the site that is now Toronto's Hospital for Sick Children? A bust and historical plaque on University Avenue today mark her birthplace.

What is Canada's longest running one-hour TV drama?

That distinction goes to CBC's *Heartland*, which aired its 125th episode in October 2014, surpassing the previous number one, *Street Legal*, which aired from 1987 to 1994. At the time of writing, *Heartland* is still going strong after 161 episodes. The show takes place in the fictional town of Hudson, but it is filmed in the Alberta town of High River, just south of Calgary. Maggie's Diner, a major location on the show, was destroyed in the flooding that hit the High River area in June 2013. The show donated eighty thousand dollars they had raised to help with rebuilding efforts.

What is the longest running Canadian comedy-drama series of all time?

That would be *The Beachcombers*, starring Bruno Gerussi, which ran from 1972 to 1990. In all, 387 episodes were produced. In 2002 a TV movie sequel was made, even though Gerussi and co-star Robert Clothier had long since died.

Who are the only two Canadians who have won the Nobel Prize for Literature?

The two recipients of the award came almost forty years apart. The first to win the esteemed prize was Saul Bellow, from Lachine, Quebec, in 1976. His best-known works include *The Adventures of Augie March*, *Henderson the Rain King*, *Herzog*, *Mr. Sammler's Planet*, *Seize the Day*, *Humboldt's Gift*, and *Ravelstein*. And more recently, acclaimed writer Alice Munroe was honoured with the prize in 2013 for her body of work, which includes the novel *Lives of Girls and Women* and the short story "The Bear Came over the Mountain," which was adapted for the screen as *Away from Her*, directed by Canadian director Sarah Polley. In addition to her Nobel honour, Munroe over her long and impressive career has won three Governor General's Awards (1968, 1978, 1986), two Giller Prizes (1998, 2004), and the Man Booker International Prize (2009).

?

DID YOU KNOW ...

that the bestselling book by a Canadian author of all time is *Anne of Green Gables* by Lucy Maud Montgomery, which has sold more than fifty million copies since it was published in 1908?

How did a Canadian bear become the inspiration for A.A. Milne's Winnie-the-Pooh?

A black bear cub from Canada named Winnipeg ("Winnie," for short) was one of the most popular attractions at the London Zoo after it was donated to the zoo in 1915. The bear cub had been bought from a hunter for twenty dollars by Canadian Lieutenant Harry Colebourn in White River, Ontario, while he was on his way to England during the First World War. Winnie became a favourite of Christopher Robin Milne when he visited the zoo, and the young boy named his own teddy bear after the real bear. This then inspired the stories written by his father, A.A. Milne, about Winnie-the-Pooh. One interesting fact: The Latin translation of *Winnie-the-Pooh*, titled *Winnie ille Pu* (1958), became the only Latin book ever to make the *New York Times* Best Sellers list.

What popular board game was created by Canadians?

The game of Trivial Pursuit was created in December 1979 in Montreal by Canadians Chris Haney and Scott Abbott and first released in 1982. Since then it has been a staple of board game and trivia aficionados everywhere. In 1984 alone twenty million games were sold. As of 2014 more than one hundred million games had been sold in twenty-six countries and in seventeen languages.

What is the bestselling album by a Canadian artist of all time?

The ladies have it here. Shania Twain's *Come On Over*, released in 1997, has sold more than forty million copies, making it twelfth in the world for all-time sales. Not far behind is 1995's *Jagged Little Pill* by Alanis Morissette at more than thirty-three million copies and two by Celine Dion, 1996's *Falling Into You* and 1997's *Let's Talk About Love*, with sales of thirty-two million and thirty-one million plus, respectively. Dion is the only female recording artist to have two albums with more than thirty million copies sold. And the bestselling album of all time? Michael Jackson's *Thriller*, of course, with worldwide sales topping 110 million!

THE OLD BALL GAME

Which Canadian professional sports team played their first major league game in the snow?

After the National League's successful expansion into Canada with the Montreal Expos in 1969, the American League decided to go international, as well, adding the Toronto Blue Jays for the 1977 season.

The weather proved unco-operative, and snow blanketed the field at Toronto's Exhibition Stadium for the scheduled home opener on April 7. But the Blue Jays organization was determined to get the first game in, and the Jays and Chicago White Sox took to the field in weather that may have resulted in a postponement on any other day, in any other city. The Jays won their franchise opener 9–5 on the strength of two home runs by Doug Ault.

Where was the first retractable dome stadium in Canada?

When Montreal's Olympic Stadium was first built, the plan was for it to have a retractable roof operated from an inclined tower. Labour disruptions and design problems prevented the roof from being ready in time for the 1976 Summer Olympic Games, or for the building's use as the home of the Montreal Expos.

When the city of Toronto began building the retractable SkyDome (now known as the Rogers Centre) for the Blue Jays, Montreal pushed to finally get its retractable roof in place before its Canadian rivals, and in 1988 Olympic Stadium became the first retractable-dome stadium in the majors; SkyDome followed a year later.

The convertible era in Montreal was short-lived, however. The roof was difficult to operate, prone to ripping, and unsuitable for use in high winds. After three seasons the roof was permanently affixed.

How many pitchers for Canadian baseball teams have thrown a perfect game?

Dennis Martínez is the only pitcher for a Canadian team to throw a perfect game. He threw to twenty-seven batters in a game against the Los Angeles Dodgers on July 28, 1991, which the Montreal Expos won 2–0. Dave Stieb was pitching for the Toronto Blue Jays in 1988, when he became one of only two pitchers to give up a hit to the twenty-seventh batter after retiring the first twenty-six (in fact, he did it a total of three times). He went on to lose the game.

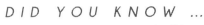

DID YOU KNOW ...
that Dave Stieb is the one and only Blue Jays pitcher to ever throw a no-hitter, accomplishing the feat on September 2, 1990, against the Cleveland Indians?

What was the first non-American team in the major leagues?

The first major league team outside the United States was the Montreal Expos, or as they were known to hometown fans, *Les Expos de Montréal*. The Expos were formed in 1969, and their name refers to the 1967 Universal and International Exposition, or Expo 67 as it was commonly known, the World's Fair held in Montreal, Canada, from April 28 to October 27, 1967. After the 2004 season the franchise was relocated by Major League Baseball (its owners since 2002) to Washington, D.C., and became the Washington Nationals.

Who is Youppi!?

Youppi! is the giant, shaggy, orange-haired creature that was mascot of the Montreal Expos for twenty-five years. The costume was designed by Bonnie Erickson, formerly a designer for Jim Henson, and the creator of Miss Piggy, Statler and Waldorf, and other Muppets. After the Expos moved to Washington, D.C., Montreal's NHL team, the Canadiens, bought Youppi! in a reported six-figure deal, making Youppi! the first mascot in pro sports to switch leagues.

DID YOU KNOW ...
that during the Expos' longest game ever — a twenty-two-inning marathon that they lost against the Los Angeles Dodgers on August 23, 1989 — Montreal's mascot Youppi! jumped noisily on the roof of the Dodgers' dugout in the eleventh inning, and L.A. manager Tommy Lasorda complained to the umpire, causing Youppi! to become the first team mascot ever to be ejected from a game?

Who did the Montreal Expos face in their first and last games?

Coincidentally, the Expos played both their first and last games against the same team, the New York Mets. On April 8, 1969, the newly formed Montreal squad made their professional debut at Shea Stadium, where they defeated the Mets 11–10. Thirty-five years later they ended their run in the same stadium, losing to the Mets 8–1 on October 3, 2004.

Why did the Expos unfurl a banner commemorating their 1994 team at their final home game?

In August 1994 the Montreal Expos were in first place with a record of 74–40 and showed every sign that they would advance to the postseason for only the second time in their career. The Major League Baseball Players Association had other plans, however, as the players went on strike on August 12, bringing the season to a premature close, and resulting in the cancellation of the entire postseason, including the World Series. At their final home game on September 29, 2004, Montreal unfurled a banner reading "1994 Meilleure Équipe du Baseball/Best Team in Baseball," commemorating their 1994 team. Ironically, the only time the Expos actually did make it to the postseason was in 1981, another year shortened by — though not completely lost to — a players' strike.

How did the Toronto Blue Jays get their name?

While Toronto is indeed in blue jay territory, the pesky, screeching birds that can be seen throughout the metropolis in the summer were only a convenient marketing device for Labatt Breweries, the initial majority owner of the city's Major League Baseball team. While a contest was held to name the new team, "Blue Jays" was eventually chosen by Labatt Breweries because Labatt's Blue was (and remains) its premier brand of beer, which was sold at ball games. The brewery had hoped Torontonians would call their team "The Blues," for short, but locals opted instead for "The Jays."

What is the highest-scoring game in World Series history?

In game four of the 1993 World Series between the Toronto Blue Jays and Philadelphia Phillies, home team Philadelphia was up 14–9 in the top of the eighth, when the Blue Jays rallied to score six runs on hits from Paul Molitor, Tony Fernández, Rickey Henderson, and Devon White. The Jays took the game 15–14, and the game remains the highest scoring in the history of the World Series.

Has the MLB All-Star game ever been played outside the United States?

The All-Star Game has been played outside the United States only twice, both times on Canadian soil. On July 13, 1982, the Montreal Expos hosted the All-Star Game at Olympic Stadium. The National League won 4–1 before a crowd of 59,057. The second time was in Toronto, on July 9, 1991, as the Blue Jays hosted the Midsummer Classic at the SkyDome (now Rogers Centre). The American League won 4–2 in front of 52,383 fans.

DID YOU KNOW ...
that in 1993, Blue Jays John Olerud, Robbie Alomar, and Paul Molitor finished 1-2-3 in the major league batting race — the first time teammates had done so in one hundred years?

GRIDIRON

HISTORY

Who was the Grey Cup
named after?

- -

Albert Henry George Grey, fourth Earl Grey, was governor general of Canada from 1904 to 1911. In 1909 he sought to cement his legacy by donating a sports trophy.

Originally, the plan was to award the Grey Cup to the champion amateur senior hockey team in the country. However, Sir Hugh Andrew Montagu Allan got in the way by donating the Allan Cup — a trophy still awarded to this day. The Grey Cup was then designated for the amateur rugby football champion.

Unfortunately, Earl Grey was a little slow about getting the trophy ready. When the University of Toronto won the first Grey Cup game that December, no trophy was present. The championship team was not awarded the Grey Cup until March 1910.

?

DID YOU KNOW ...
that the University of Toronto Varsity Blues and Queen's University are the only teams to have won both the Grey Cup and the Vanier Cup? The Grey Cup was originally contested by amateur teams. U of T won four Grey Cups, while Queen's won three. Later the Vanier Cup became Canada's university championship.

How many American cities have fielded teams in the Canadian Football League (CFL)?

In total, seven American cities have been part of the CFL.

In the 1990s the CFL embarked on a grand experiment to expand into the United States. The first U.S.-based team, the Sacramento Gold Miners, took the field in 1993. The following season they were joined by teams from Baltimore, Las Vegas, and Shreveport, Louisiana. By 1995 the expansion was struggling, and the Las Vegas team folded, while the Sacramento team moved to San Antonio. Other teams were added in Memphis and Birmingham, Alabama, with little success.

After two seasons of American expansion, all but the Baltimore Stallions and San Antonio Texans had called it quits. The Stallions — upon learning that the NFL's Cleveland Browns were moving to Baltimore — relocated to Montreal, becoming the latest incarnation of the Alouettes. The Texans, unenthused at the prospect of playing the lone American team in a league based in a country more than 2,414 kilometres away, ceased operations.

What was the most successful American team in the CFL?

The CFL's American expansion began in 1993, but the most successful franchise to play south of the border did not take the field until 1994. The Baltimore Stallions, who played out of the city's aging Memorial Stadium, burst out of the gates in their first season with a 12–6 regular season record, then advanced to the Grey Cup, where they lost on a last-second field goal by Lui Passaglia.

In 1995 the team was even better, putting together a 15–3 record and returning to the Grey Cup, where they became the first, and last, American team to win Canada's football championship, defeating the Calgary Stampeders by a score of 37–20. The following year, when the Stallions moved to Montreal, they were the only American franchise to survive the collapse of the CFL's ambitious experiment.

What CFL team played without a name during its first season?

When the city of Baltimore was granted a CFL franchise for the 1994 season, owner Jim Speros wanted to name the team the Baltimore Colts — which was the name of the city's original NFL franchise. The NFL, which held the rights to the name, took legal action, winning an injunction.

Stuck without a name the team was referred to as the Baltimore CFLers and the Baltimore Football Club, but had no official name. As an act of defiance, the team's public address announcer would introduce the team as "Your Baltimore … " allowing the spectators to shout out "Colts."

After the season fans were given a chance to vote for a new name for the team. The winning name was "Stallions."

Who came first, the Ottawa Rough Riders or the Saskatchewan Roughriders?

It was long a source of amusement that the CFL had two teams with nearly identical names — the *Rough Riders* and the *Roughriders*. Both claimed to be the "true" Riders, but the fact is, Ottawa was the first to use the name.

The Ottawa team was first established in 1876 as a member of the Ontario Amateur Athletic Association. For twenty-one years it played as the Ottawa Football Club, until adopting the name "Rough Riders" in 1897. The name was a reference to the log rollers who would ride the logs on the rough local rivers.

By the 1920s East-West matches were commonplace, and the Regina Rugby Club took to the field in 1921. Three years later the Ottawa franchise temporarily changed its name to the Senators (1925–30), and the Regina club snatched up the name, squeezing it into one word, *Roughriders*. (There are two theories about the origins of their version of the name: one theory contends the Regina team named itself after the North West Mounted Police, who were known as "roughriders" for their ability to break wild horses; the other argues that the team was named after a Canadian regiment that fought in the Spanish-American War.)

The team played as the Regina Roughriders until 1948, when teams in Moose Jaw and Saskatoon folded and the Regina team came under the ownership of the province. Since that time they have been known as the Saskatchewan Roughriders.

Ottawa's team brought back the name Rough Riders in 1931 and that name stuck until the team folded in 1996. They re-emerged as the Renegades in 2001, but that team only lasted until 2006. The current Ottawa franchise, the Redblacks, joined the league in 2014 and won the Grey Cup in 2016.

How many times has the CFL staged an All-Star Game?

The CFL All-Star Game has had an on-again, off-again existence since the 1950s. The game was played for four consecutive years, from 1955 to 1958, and then shelved. It was reborn in 1970 and had a steady run until 1978.

Two attempts were made to revive the game. In 1983 the Eastern and Western conferences squared off at B.C. Place Stadium in Vancouver. In 1988 the league experimented with a format they'd tried in the early seventies, matching the Grey Cup champions (the Edmonton Eskimos) against a team of league all-stars.

In total, fourteen all-star games have been played. While the game is no longer held, the CFL continues to release an annual list of all-stars.

?

DID YOU KNOW ...
that during the Second World War there was a shortage of men to play professional sports, so military units often competed instead? Between 1942 and 1944, Grey Cup games were contested between service teams.

?

DID YOU KNOW ...
that James Naismith, the inventor of basketball, is sometimes credited with inventing the original football helmet?

How many Eastern Division Championships have the Winnipeg Blue Bombers won?

- -

Though traditionally a Western team, major changes have led to the Winnipeg Blue Bombers playing in the CFL's Eastern Division on numerous occasions.

After the collapse of the Montreal Alouettes in 1987, the league moved the Bombers from the West to the East in order to avoid a three-team Eastern Division. Football returned to Montreal in 1995, and the Bombers moved back to the West. The stay didn't last long, however, as the Ottawa Rough Riders folded, and Winnipeg became an Eastern Division city again in 1997.

Ottawa briefly returned to the CFL with the Renegades from 2002 to 2005, causing another shift back to the West, but the failure of that franchise led to the return of Winnipeg to the East in 2006. But alas, when the Ottawa Redblacks joined the league in 2014, Winnipeg was again shifted back to the Western Division.

During their time as an Eastern Division team, the Winnipeg Blue Bombers have won seven division championships, in 1988, 1990, 1992, 1993, 2001, 2007, and 2011. Only one of those championships — in 1990 — was converted into a Grey Cup championship.

What major brewery named its most popular beer after a football team?

Labatt's cornerstone beer began life in the early 1950s as "Labatt's Pilsner Lager." But the beer's distinct blue label led Winnipeg Blue Bombers fans to calling the beer "Blue," after their football team. The name eventually stuck, and it became the official name of the brew, which is one of the bestselling beers in Canada.

Labatt's later became affiliated with another "Blue" team as the original owners of the Toronto Blue Jays. Unfortunately for the Labatt's marketing department, both "Blue" teams are commonly referred to by the colourless short-forms of their names: the Bombers and the Jays.

Who owned both the Hamilton Tiger-Cats and the Toronto Maple Leafs?

Torontonians already had a dislike for Harold Ballard, whose ownership of hockey's Toronto Maple Leafs had been, and would remain, chaotic and controversial for years. Then, in 1978, Ballard bought the fledgling Hamilton Tiger-Cats — the hated rivals of the Toronto Argonauts. To make matters worse the Tiger-Cats, under Ballard, appeared in four Grey Cups, winning once, while the Toronto Maple Leafs were in the middle of a prolonged Stanley Cup drought.

Not that Hamiltonians were any fonder of Ballard and his antics. He once referred to the Tiger-Cats as a "bunch of overpaid losers." Later that year — after the Tiger-Cats won the Grey Cup — he admitted that they were "worth every penny."

How many teams have gone undefeated in a CFL season?

Perfect seasons have been tough to come by in the CFL, particularly in the modern era of twenty-game seasons. Only one team has pulled it off in CFL history, and even that perfection is debatable.

The 1948 Calgary Stampeders finished the regular season with a 12–0 record. At the time Calgary was a member of the Western Interprovincial Football Union, which played its championships under a two-game total-points format. The teams tied the first game 4–4, and Calgary won the second 21–10. While the tie would seem to mar the perfect record, the total-points format meant that neither game could be considered a win, loss, or tie on its own.

Following the win, Calgary went on to the Grey Cup and defeated the Ottawa Rough Riders 12–7.

How many incarnations of the Montreal Alouettes have there been?

Three different Montreal teams have gone by the name "Alouettes." The first, founded in 1872, adopted the name Alouettes (French for "lark") in 1946. This incarnation was forced to fold after the 1981 season, when team owner Nelson Skalbania — who had only purchased the team a year earlier — filed for bankruptcy as his financial empire collapsed.

The following season Charles Bronfman revived football in Montreal with a new team, called the Concordes. In 1986 the Concordes, struggling to gain fan support, dipped into the past and renamed itself the Alouettes. A year later the team folded.

Finally, when the CFL's American experiment failed, the Baltimore Stallions moved to Montreal in 1996 and were immediately renamed the Alouettes.

DID YOU KNOW ...
that Halifax was granted a CFL franchise in 1984 (the Atlantic Schooners), but the team folded before ever playing a game because it couldn't finance a new stadium?

What Canadian university football team was part of U.S. college football until 2002?

The National Association of Intercollegiate Athletics (NAIA) differs from the NCAA in that it is an association of smaller colleges, and it allows international entries. The Simon Fraser University Clan, wanting to compete in a system that allowed full scholarships (which were not permitted in Canada at the time) joined the NAIA in 1965, and it continued to play in the American system until joining the Canadian Interuniversity Sport in 2002.

How did the Hamilton Tiger-Cats get the hyphenated name?

The early history of football in Hamilton, Ontario, is a story of mergers. The original Hamilton Tigers coexisted with the Hamilton Alerts in the early 1900s and won five Grey Cups between 1913 and 1932. During the Second World War a separate team, the Hamilton Flying Wildcats, emerged and won the 1943 Grey Cup.

But in the postwar era the two teams found themselves in financial difficulties, due to the fact that they were competing for the same fan base. So in 1950 they merged. They combined their names into "Tiger-Cats." For some time they also combined team colours — the black and yellow of the Tigers were joined by the red, white, and blue of the Flying Wildcats. Over time the overkill of colours was pared down to the current black, yellow, and white.

What Canadian football player was the coveted trophy in a season of *The Bachelor*?

Canadian quarterback Jesse Palmer had brief stints with the New York Giants and San Francisco 49ers in the NFL and the Montreal Alouettes in the CFL. But his greatest fame came when he starred in the American reality show *The Bachelor*. After narrowing down his dating options (at one point forgetting a woman's name mid-dump), Palmer settled on Jessica Bowlin. Unfortunately, as is usually the case with romance that blooms on *The Bachelor*, the relationship was short-lived and the two soon parted ways.

Why is a touchdown worth six points?

In an early form of the game, teams could only score by kicking. When a touchdown was made, it only allowed a team to kick for a point. (Points could also be scored by kicking without the benefit of a touchdown.)

In the early 1880s it was decided that touchdowns should be more valuable than kicks from the field, and a points system was introduced. At first a touchdown counted as four points, and the subsequent kick was worth another four points. Then, in 1897, the value of a touchdown increased to five points, while the kick after was reduced to a single point.

The touchdown became worth six points in American football in 1912. Canadian football stuck with the traditional five points until 1956, when the touchdown increased from five to six points.

When was instant replay introduced as a means of reviewing calls in the CFL?

While instant replay had been in use off and on in the NFL since 1986, and regularly since 1999, the CFL's board of governors did not approve the officiating aid until 2006.

What is a "rouge" in Canadian football?

While fans of the Canadian game rarely use the term *rouge* nowadays, the word is still used in the official rules.

A rouge is a single point that is scored when a ball is either kicked through the end zone, or kicked into the end zone and not returned past the goal line by the receiving team. This can occur on punts, missed field goal attempts, or kickoffs. A point after a touchdown is not considered a "rouge," nor is the three-point field goal.

The rouge, also known as a single, is unique to the Canadian game. It is not clear how the word *rouge* came to be applied to the score.

Why is Canadian football considered a "passing" game, while American football is considered a "running" game?

The rules and the size of the playing field have made the Canadian game a haven for the quarterback who loves big passing plays.

With only three downs to work with, short yardage gains put Canadian teams in down trouble, meaning that the grind-it-out tactic often employed by American teams to gain a few yards at a time on the ground is risky.

Also, the Canadian field is much larger than the American field. It's longer, 110 yards from goal line to goal line, with 20-yard end zones, making it a total of 30 yards longer than the American field. It's also wider, measuring 65 yards from sideline to sideline, compared to the 53 1/3-yard width of American fields. With so much more room, passing plays are more difficult to defend against.

Who is the CFL's all-time pass king?

On October 28, 2000, Damon Allen of the B.C. Lions made a 45-yard touchdown pass to Alfred Jackson that moved him past the legendary Russ Jackson into sole possession of first place in the CFL's all-time passing yards list. Allen went on to become the most prolific passer in professional football history. However, his record was surpassed in 2011 by Anthony Calvillo. During his CFL career, spent with the Tiger-Cats and Alouettes, Calvillo passed for 79,816 yards and is one of seven professional quarterbacks to have completed over four hundred touchdown passes. He is now coaching with the Montreal Alouettes (2016–17).

Who is the only player elected to both the Pro Football Hall of Fame and the Canadian Football Hall of Fame?

Many players have had success in both the NFL and the CFL, but none have been as accomplished in both leagues as Warren Moon.

After a solid college career Moon went undrafted by the NFL, and he had to look north of the border for work. He joined the Edmonton Eskimos and quickly became one of the most dominant players in league history, leading his team to five consecutive Grey Cup wins between 1978 and 1982.

Moon then converted his CFL success into NFL interest and signed with the Houston Oilers. While Moon never made it to the Super Bowl, he became one of only two quarterbacks to pass for more than 4,000 yards in consecutive seasons, and he was named to the Pro Bowl nine times.

When he retired, his combined totals in the CFL and the NFL established several professional football records, including most career passing yards and most career passing touchdowns. He was elected to the Canadian Football Hall of Fame in 2001 and the Pro Football Hall of Fame in 2006.

Which CFL player was known as "The Little General"?

Though he was only five foot five, Ron Lancaster became a Canadian football legend. Known for his leadership and play-calling abilities, he earned the nickname "The Little General."

Lancaster spent the first three years of his CFL career with the Ottawa Rough Riders before being traded to the Saskatchewan Roughriders before the 1963 season. He spent sixteen seasons with Saskatchewan, leading the team to five Grey Cup appearances, including one win.

After his playing career Lancaster built on his "Little General" reputation as a head coach, winning Grey Cups in Edmonton and Hamilton.

Who passed up an opportunity to interview for a Rhodes Scholarship in order to play in the CFL?

An all-around athlete, excelling in multiple sports, McMaster University's Russ Jackson was also a gifted academic. In 1958 he was his school's nominee for a Rhodes Scholarship.

However, Jackson felt the pull of professional football, and he declined to interview for the scholarship, electing instead to sign with the Ottawa Rough Riders.

Who declared, "It will take an act of God to beat us on Saturday" prior to a 1969 CFL playoff game?

The Toronto Argonauts faced the Ottawa Rough Riders in the two-game total-points Eastern Division final in 1969. The Argos won the first game handily 22–14. Coach Leo Cahill, confident that his team had Ottawa's number, despite the fact that they had only beaten the Rough Riders twice in their last twelve encounters, told the media that "It will take an act of God to beat us on Saturday."

That weekend the act of God actually occurred. The field at Ottawa's Lansdowne Park was frozen, and the Argos were only equipped with standard cleats and running shoes. The Rough Riders, meanwhile, had broomball-style shoes that provided excellent traction on the slippery surface. The Rough Riders pounded the Argos 32–3 to advance to the Grey Cup.

Who did the Calgary Stampeders ban from a playoff game against the Saskatchewan Roughriders in 2006?

The Calgary Stampeders were surprised by the outrage when they decided to ban Gainer the Gopher, the mascot of the Saskatchewan Roughriders, from entering McMahon Stadium for the 2006 Western Division semifinal. Stamps' president Ted Hellard said the move was for the good of the Stamps' own mascot, Ralph the Dog.

"Our fans," he said, "have earned the right for us to be led on the field by our own mascot without competition from Gainer." Gainer had the last laugh, though — albeit from a province away. The Roughriders overcame a sixteen-point deficit to defeat the Stampeders 30–21.

What was memorable about the 1948 Grey Cup?

The fact that the Calgary Stampeders won the 1948 Grey Cup in Toronto and completed a perfect season is almost a side note. The game itself featured memorable moments, such as the "sitting touchdown," a trick play in which receiver Norm Hill lay on his back in the end zone, virtually hidden, then sat up to receive the touchdown pass. But the real excitement occurred at the Royal York Hotel, where celebrating Stampeders fans carried the goalposts into the lobby and rode horses through the front doors and onto the elevators.

Which team has won the most Grey Cups?

If we count the entire history of the Grey Cup, including the years prior to the CFL when amateur teams competed for the trophy, the Toronto Argonauts lead the pack with sixteen Grey Cup wins.

It is generally felt, though, that the modern era of Canadian football didn't begin until the mid 1950s, by which time the championship was played exclusively between professional teams in the organizations that, a few years later, became known as the Canadian Football League.

Beginning in 1954 the Edmonton Eskimos have been the winningest team in Grey Cup history, taking the trophy home fourteen times.

When was the first Grey Cup played?

On December 4, 1909, the University of Toronto met the Parkdale Canoe Club at Rosedale field to determine the Rugby Football Championship of Canada. Although Lord Earl Grey's trophy was not ready yet, it had already been determined that the winner of this game would be the inaugural recipient of the Grey Cup. Led by kicker Hugh Gall, who kicked a record eight singles, the University of Toronto team prevailed by a score of 26–6 before a crowd of 3,807.

When was the first Vanier Cup played?

When originally conceived, the Vanier Cup was the name of the trophy awarded to the winner of the Canadian College Bowl. The idea was similar to American college bowl games: two teams would be invited by a panel to play for what was being called the "national championship," despite the absence of a playoff system.

The first winner of the Vanier Cup was the University of Toronto, who defeated the University of Alberta 14–7 at Toronto's Varsity Stadium.

After two years the game came under the direction of the Canadian Interuniversity Athletic Union (CIAU — until 2016 known as Canadian Interuniversity Sport and now as U Sport). A playoff system was developed, and the invitation format was abandoned. The first winner under the new playoff system was the University of Alberta, who triumphed 10–9 over McMaster University.

Who has won the most Vanier Cups?

The University of Laval Rouge et Or has won the trophy a staggering nine times, with its first victory coming in 1999, and it is one of the powerhouses of Canadian football. The other wins came in 2003, 2004, 2006, 2008, 2010, 2012, 2013, and 2016, all under current head coach Glen Constantin.

What Canadian player has scored the most points in the CFL?

Vancouver-born Lui Passaglia is not only the all-time leader among Canadians, but he has also scored more points than any player in any professional sports league. In 408 career games as place-kicker and punter — all with the BC Lions — Passaglia amassed 3,991 points.

Passaglia's most famous moment came in the 1994 Grey Cup, when he kicked a cup-winning field goal on the last play of the game.

Who is the coach with the most wins in CFL history?

On September 19, 2009, Wally Buono became the CFL's all-time winningest coach when his BC Lions beat the Toronto Argonauts 23–17, giving him 232 regular-season victories, surpassing Don Matthews's total. By the end of the 2016 season, Buono had amassed 269 wins with the Calgary Stampeders (1990–2002) and the BC Lions (2003–11, 2016).

Where was the one hundreth Grey Cup game played?

On November 26, 2012, the CFL celebrated the one hundredth anniversary of the Grey Cup, with the game taking place in Toronto — the forty-sixth time the city had hosted the championship game. In the lead-up to the big game, the league launched The Grey Cup 100 Train Tour, which include three CFL-themed railway coaches, which criss-crossed the country for ten weeks, pulling in to Toronto nine days prior to the game. The train featured a museum car, a railcar containing modern CFL memorabilia, and a car carrying the Grey Cup itself. The game featured the hometown Argonauts taking on the Calgary Stampeders. In the end the home team emerged victorious in a 35–22 win.

DID YOU KNOW ...

that the 1968 Grey Cup was the last one played on a Saturday? The following year the game was moved to Sunday and has remained there ever since.

THE SUPER SIX: GREATEST GREY CUP PLAYS

1. Tom Clements to Tony Gabriel, 1976 Grey Cup

This battle between the two Riders teams also pitted two future Hall of Fame quarterbacks against each other: the Saskatchewan Roughriders' Ron Lancaster, and the Ottawa Rough Riders' Tom Clements. But late in the game it looked like the Saskatchewan defence might be the stars of the game, as a goal line stand forced Ottawa to turn the ball over on downs with less than two minutes to play and Saskatchewan ahead 20-16.

Then it was Ottawa's turn to come up big as the team got the ball back into the hands of Clements. With twenty seconds to play, Clements sent Tony Gabriel long. Gabriel faked a post pattern, then ran toward the corner of the end zone, where Clements hit him with a 24-yard touchdown pass to win the Grey Cup.

2. Ken Ploen, 1961 Grey Cup

Grey Cups have a history of being tight contests, but the 1961 final was unique in that it went into overtime, and it has been called one of the greatest Grey Cups ever played.

Ken Ploen, in his fifth year as a quarterback with the Winnipeg Blue Bombers, was midway through a Hall of Fame career when he pulled off one of the most memorable touchdown runs in the championship's history. With just over six minutes to play in overtime, he called his own number and scampered around a host of Hamilton Tiger-Cats defenders for an 18-yard touchdown run that lifted the Bombers to the team's third Grey Cup in four years.

3. Vic Washington, 1968 Grey Cup

With the Ottawa Rough Riders trailing the Calgary Stampeders 14-10 in the fourth quarter, Ottawa was looking to gain some ground. The play that turned things around for them was nearly a disaster.

Running back Vic Washington took the hand-off and had a free route down the sideline, but worried about his footing (the ground was muddy), he fumbled the ball. Fortunately for Washington, the fumble bounced back into his hands, and he completed his touchdown run — a 79-yard run from scrimmage that remains a Grey Cup record.

After this play the teams exchanged touchdowns, and Ottawa won the game 24–21.

4. Anthony Calvillo to Pat Woodcock, 2002 Grey Cup

The newest version of the Montreal Alouettes had won a Grey Cup in 1995, but were playing in Baltimore at the time. The city of Montreal had not won the championship since 1977.

In the second quarter the Als made a statement with the longest touchdown reception in Grey Cup history. Anthony Calvillo, at his own 11, took the snap and found a wide-open Pat Woodcock at the 40. Woodcock eluded the grasp of an Edmonton defender and ran 70 more yards for the touchdown — a total of 99 yards on the play.

The Alouettes went on to win the game 26–16.

5. Henry "Gizmo" Williams, 1987 Grey Cup

The Edmonton Eskimos won the 1987 Grey Cup over the Toronto Argonauts on a last-second field goal by Jerry Kauric, but the most spectacular play of the game came in the first quarter.

Argos kicker Lance Chomyc missed on a field goal attempt, which was caught by Henry "Gizmo" Williams five yards deep in the end zone. Williams brought the ball out, dodged Argos tacklers, headed to the sidelines, and turned upfield. He was untouched the rest of the way as he completed a Grey Cup-record 115-yard return for a touchdown. The Eskimos won the game 38–36, and Damon Allen was named MVP, but Williams's run was the highlight that endured.

6. Eddie Brown, 1996 Grey Cup

For a play to be considered "great" when it comes in the first quarter, and it is pulled off by a member of the losing team, it has to be something special. In the snowy 1996 Grey Cup, Edmonton Eskimos' quarterback Danny McManus hurled a frozen football toward receiver "Downtown" Eddie Brown running up the sideline. The ball was just within Brown's reach, but pulling the rock-hard ball in was not going to be an easy feat. It bounced off his fingers, then off his knee, and Brown reached down to snare the ball off his shoestrings. He never broke stride, and he took the ball to the end zone for a 64-yard score.

The Eskimos took a 9-0 lead on the play, but Doug Flutie and the Toronto Argonauts would go on to win the game 43-37.

CANADA'S GAME

Who made the first hockey sticks?

The First Nations connection to the very first hockey sticks got a boost in early 2008, when the son of a Quebec City antique dealer acquired what he claims is a 350-year-old curved Mi'kmaq stick that he says proves aboriginal people played hockey in Canada as early as the late seventeenth century. The man's assertion hasn't met with much support among experts, but one thing is certain: the Mi'kmaq of Nova Scotia were carving single-piece hockey sticks at least as early as the 1870s and probably earlier. They utilized a wood known as hornbeam (also called ironwood) because of its strength. Later they turned to yellow birch, when they exhausted the available hornbeam. These early sticks curved up like field hockey sticks and were much shorter and heavier than the kind used in modern ice hockey. The Starr Manufacturing Company in Dartmouth, Nova Scotia, started producing hockey sticks in the late nineteenth century under the brand names Mic-Mac and Rex. The company's sticks were immensely popular well into the 1930s.

?

DID YOU KNOW ...
that the world's largest hockey stick is in Duncan, British Columbia, on Vancouver Island? The 62.48-metre, 28,120-kilogram wooden stick once adorned the entrance to Vancouver's Expo 86. The stick has been recognized officially in *Guinness World Records* as the planet's largest.

DID YOU KNOW ...
that Montreal's Victoria Skating Rink opened for business in 1862, was the first building in Canada to be electrified, and was the scene of the first Stanley Cup playoff game in 1894? The arena closed for good in 1937. Today a parking garage sits on the site.

Why is Kingston, Ontario, thought by many to be the birthplace of hockey?

The first recorded games of shinny on ice were played in Kingston, Upper Canada, in 1839. A British Army officer, Arthur Freeling, said he and fellow soldiers played "hockey on the ice" in January 1843 in Kingston. Edward Horsey, in his diary, noted that shinny was played on the ice of Kingston's harbour in the 1860s by soldiers. However, an organized game with rules wasn't played in Kingston until 1886. That match pitted Queen's College students against Royal Military College cadets and occurred eleven years after the first recorded indoor game in Montreal.

When was the first organized hockey team founded in Canada?

On January 31, 1877, McGill University students started the first organized ice hockey club. Employing codified rules, hockey officials, and team uniforms, the McGill University Hockey Club played a challenge match against a loose collection of lacrosse and football players. McGill beat its opponents 2–1.

What teams were involved in the world's first hockey championship?

In 1883 at Montreal's inaugural Winter Carnival, the world's first hockey championship was held, pitting three teams against one another: the Montreal Victorias, the McGill University Hockey Club, and a team from Quebec City. The three teams vied for the sterling silver Carnival Cup. McGill University won the series. The championship was restaged at the carnival in 1884 and 1885.

?

DID YOU KNOW ...

that the second organized hockey team in history was the Montreal Victorias, which debuted in 1881 and later went on to win the Stanley Cup in 1895, holding it from that year until 1899 (except for a challenge loss to the Winnipeg Victorias in 1896), when the team lost it for good to the Montreal Shamrocks?

When was the first game in the National Hockey League played?

The first two games in the spanking new National Hockey League were played on December 19, 1917. The Montreal Wanderers edged the Toronto Arenas 10–9, and the Montreal Canadiens defeated the Ottawa Senators 7–4. The Wanderers' match only attracted seven hundred fans. Unfortunately for the Wanderers, once one of the greatest hockey teams and winners of the Stanley Cup four times, its arena burned down two weeks later, and the franchise folded.

Who is Peter Puck?

The hockey puck–shaped cartoon character Peter Puck was dreamed up by the National Broadcasting Company and was developed for television by NBC and Hanna-Barbera. He took his first bow on the American network on NBC's *Hockey Game of the Week* in 1973. The cartoon creature, whose voice was provided by actor Ronnie Schell, explained hockey rules and equipment and informed a primarily U.S. audience about the game's rules and history. The nine original NBC episodes were each about three minutes long and were broadcast between NHL hockey game periods. When NBC stopped broadcasting NHL games in 1975, it sold the rights to Peter Puck to Hanna-Barbera, which in turn sold them to prolific hockey writer and broadcaster Brian McFarlane, who still controls the animated figure. McFarlane had been part of the broadcast team for NBC's hockey games in the 1970s, was involved in the creation of Peter, and continued running less-expensive Peter Puck sequences on CBC's *Hockey Night in Canada* until 1980. Three Peter Puck books were spawned by McFarlane from1975 to 1980: *Peter Puck: Love That Hockey Game!*, *Peter Puck and the Stolen Stanley Cup*, and *Peter Puck's Greatest Moments in Hockey*. Some merchandise was also produced, including a fondly remembered colouring book. The plucky Peter staged something of a comeback during the 2007 NHL Playoffs, with merchandise sporting the critter and a DVD of all the 1970s episodes hitting stores. Original Peter Puck episodes began popping up in late 2007 during the first intermission of Toronto Maple Leafs games shown on Leafs TV.

What is the best children's story ever written about hockey?

In 1979 noted Quebec novelist and playwright Roch Carrier first published the short story "Une abominable feuille d'érable sur la glace" ("An Abominable Maple Leaf on the Ice"), now better known as "The Hockey Sweater" in English and "Le chandail de hockey" in French. Carrier based the story on his own experiences as a child. The narrative is simple but superb in the way it gets to the heart of the mystique of hockey for Canadians, particularly children. In the 1940s a boy's hockey sweater wears out, and his mother orders a new one from the Eaton's catalogue. The boy is a rabid fan of the Montreal Canadiens and its star forward Maurice "Rocket" Richard. However, when the new sweater finally arrives, to the boy's horror it's a Toronto Maple Leafs sweater, not a Habs one. The boy tries to get his mother to return the sweater, but she feels that Mr. Eaton, obviously a Leafs fan, might be offended, so she insists he wear the despicable Leafs garment to his hockey game. As expected the boy is the only one not wearing a Canadiens jersey. "The Hockey Sweater" is often thought to be an allegory for French and English tensions in Canada. It has been published in many forms, including a picture book for younger children. In 1980 an animated version, *The Sweater*, was released by Canada's National Film Board to much acclaim.

Who wrote the theme song for CBC-TV's *Hockey Night in Canada*?

Vancouver-born Dolores Claman wrote the theme song for *Hockey Night in Canada* (with an arrangement by Howard Cable), a ditty called "The Hockey Theme," which has become one of the most recognizable tunes ever composed in Canada. In 1968 when Claman was asked to write an anthem for the show, she supposedly had never seen a hockey game and claims she didn't actually see one in person until thirty years after the introduction of her song. The theme was first played on *Hockey Night in Canada* during the 1968–69 season. Previously, the television show's themes had been "Saturday's Game," a march by Howard Cable, and "Esso Happy Motoring Song." In 2008, after a long-standing dispute over financial compensation with CBC-TV, Claman broke with the network and signed a deal with CTV that would see "The Hockey Theme" featured on the private company's televised hockey games beginning in 2008–09.

Which Canadian invented tabletop hockey?

In 1932 Torontonian Don Munro built a model for a tabletop hockey game in his basement using scrap metal and carving hockey figures out of wood. Shortly after he sold the concept to Eaton's Department Store in Toronto, and the new game was a huge hit. Munro's largely wooden game was replaced in the mid 1950s by the Eagle Toy Company's version, which boasted painted tin figures and metal rods that allowed players to whip their hockey pieces around 360 degrees.

When did "Coach's Corner" debut on *Hockey Night in Canada*?

The bombastic, flamboyantly dressed Don Cherry made his debut on *Hockey Night in Canada* in the "Coach's Corner" segment in 1980, with Dave Hodge as his sidekick. In 1987 Hodge was replaced by Ron

MacLean, who has been Cherry's foil ever since. Always controversial, Cherry toiled in minor-league hockey as a defenceman from the 1950s to the early 1970s, finishing his playing career with the American Hockey League's Rochester Americans, a team he also coached for three seasons. He parlayed the minor-league coaching stint into a chance in the big time as head coach of the Boston Bruins, a job he held for five seasons (1974–75 to 1978–79). During the seventh game of the Stanley Cup semifinal with the Montreal Canadiens in 1979, Cherry made the mistake of allowing too many Bruins on the ice, earning a penalty for the team. The Canadiens capitalized on the error during the subsequent power play, when Guy Lafleur scored the tying goal. The match went into overtime, and the Canadiens' Yvon Lambert scored again, winning the game and eliminating Boston. The Habs went on to play the New York Rangers in the final and ended up winning the Stanley Cup. Cherry was fired. He bounced back briefly, though, in 1979–80 as head coach of the wretched Colorado Rockies, but was fired after one season.

When was hockey first broadcast on television in Canada?

Amazingly, the very first television broadcast of a hockey game occurred not in Canada but in the U.K., on October 29, 1938. The British Broadcasting Corporation (BBC) aired the second and third periods of a game between the Harringay Racers and Streatham at London's Harringay Arena. The first televised NHL game in Canada was on October 11, 1952, when *Hockey Night in Canada* debuted on the tube in French with a game at the Montreal Forum between the Chicago Black Hawks and the Montreal Canadiens called by René Lecavalier. The Habs lost to the Black Hawks 3–2. Three weeks later, on November 1, *Hockey Night in Canada* aired its first English-language broadcast — Foster Hewitt provided the play-by-play for a game between the Toronto Maple Leafs and the Boston

Bruins at Maple Leaf Gardens. The Leafs beat the Bruins 2–1. Just the last half of the game was broadcast, a policy that continued until 1968 for regular-season matches.

Which Canadian first said, "He shoots, he scores!"?

On March 22, 1923, Foster Hewitt uttered his signature "he shoots, he scores!" in his first radio broadcast, a playoff game between intermediate hockey clubs from Toronto and Kitchener at the former's Mutual Street Arena. The broadcast was done for CFCA in a glassed-in booth near the penalty box. A month before Hewitt's CFCA broadcast, on February 18, Norm Albert, an editor at the *Toronto Star*, made the very first radio broadcast of a hockey game. The senior-league match between clubs from North Toronto and Midland, Ontario, turned out to be a 16–4 blowout in favour of Toronto. On January 7, 1933, Hewitt was heard for the first time coast-to-coast on the radio when he welcomed listeners with "Hello, Canada, and hockey fans in the United States and Newfoundland" for a game between the Maple Leafs and the Detroit Red Wings, which the former won 7–6.

Who was the first Canadian hockey player to grace the cover of *Sports Illustrated*?

You would think either Maurice "Rocket" Richard or Gordie Howe would have been the first hockey player on the cover of *Sports Illustrated*, but no, it was Jean Béliveau, Richard's Montreal Canadiens teammate. Béliveau, still only twenty-four and on his way to winning his first NHL scoring title, appeared on the cover of the magazine on January 23, 1956.

?

Where did the nickname "Habs" come from to describe the Montreal Canadiens?

The Montreal Canadiens' nickname "Habs" comes from *les habitants*, a term that was once used to describe the early settlers of seventeenth- and eighteenth-century New France, the predecessor of what eventually became the province of Quebec. In fact, the Canadiens were specifically established in December 1909 in the National Hockey Association (precursor of the NHL) as a French-Canadian alternative to the many predominantly English hockey clubs in Montreal, teams such as the Shamrocks, the Wanderers, and the Victorias.

Which Canadian player holds the most records in the NHL?

With sixty NHL records in regular-season, playoff, and All-Star Games, Wayne Gretzky, of course, holds the individual record of records. Upon his retirement in 1999, the Great One actually had sixty-one records, but two of his records were eclipsed and he got one back (he also shares one record with Mike Bossy — most Fifty-or-More Goal Seasons, with nine). Gretzky's record of fifteen overtime assists has now been passed by Nicklas Lidstrom, Adam Oates, and Mark Messier, while his record of twelve All-Star Game assists has been beaten by Mark Messier, Ray Bourque, and Joe Sakic. When Mario Lemieux came out of retirement and played more games, he lost his points-per-game average record, which now belongs to Gretzky again at 1.921 points per game. Some of Gretzky's loftier records, ones that will likely never be surpassed, are: most regular-season goals (894), most regular-season assists (1,963), most regular-season points (2,857), most playoff goals (122), most goals in one season (92), and most assists in one season (163).

DID YOU KNOW ...

that "Gretzky's office" refers to the area behind a team's net? When Wayne Gretzky was on the ice, he spent a lot of time in possession of the puck behind the opposition's goal, waiting for teammates to get open in front of the net. As the Great One once commented, "When I get back there, I prefer to use a backhand pass to get the puck out front. I like to use the net as a sort of screen, to buy time from the opposing defencemen who may be trying to get me ... I try to keep the puck away from them as long as possible, so I can hopefully make a play."

Which Canadian holds the NHL record for scoring the most goals in one game?

Joe Malone of the Quebec Bulldogs scored seven goals in one game against the Toronto St. Patricks on January 31, 1920, powering his club to a 10–6 victory. Malone, born in Quebec City, was one of the NHL's first superstars. He won the scoring title twice, the first time being in the league's inaugural season in 1917–18, when he racked up forty-four goals in a mere twenty games for the Montreal Canadiens. His other scoring title came in 1919–20 with the Bulldogs. Malone won three Stanley Cups, two with Quebec (1912, 1913) and one with the Canadiens (1924). Perhaps not too surprising, he was also one of the first men to score a goal in the NHL, sharing that distinction with the Montreal Wanderers' Dave Ritchie. Both Malone and Ritchie potted goals early in their respective games on December 19, 1917. Starting times for games for the era aren't known, but Malone, a Canadien, got his goal against the Ottawa Senators early in the first period en route to beating the Sens 7–4.

What was the highest-scoring game in NHL history?

This record turns out to be a tie. On January 10, 1920, the Montreal Canadiens trounced the Toronto St. Pats 14–7. Sixty-five years later, on December 11, 1985, the Edmonton Oilers slipped by the Chicago Black Hawks 12–9. The record for most goals by one team in a single game is also held by the Canadiens, who netted sixteen against the Quebec Bulldogs' three on March 3, 1920.

Which NHL player has won the most scoring titles?

Wayne Gretzky, not too surprisingly, won ten Art Ross Trophies (1981–87, 1990, 1991, 1994), the award the NHL has given for the league's regular season scoring leader since 1947–48. Prior to that season a number of players such as Joe Malone, Newsy Lalonde, Bill Cook, and Charlie Conacher won the scoring title twice, but no single person earned it more times than that. The runners-up to Gretzky for Art Ross Trophies are Gordie Howe and Mario Lemieux, each with six. The Great One has also won the most Hart Trophies — nine — for most valuable player in the NHL during the regular season. Number 99 accomplished that feat seven seasons in a row from 1980–87, then added a ninth Hart in 1989 after he was dealt to the Los Angeles Kings.

Who holds the NHL record for the most points in one game?

On February 7, 1976, the Toronto Maple Leafs' Darryl Sittler racked up an incredible six goals and four assists for ten points in an 11–4 plastering of the Boston Bruins at Maple Leaf Gardens. That record for points still stands. Centreman Sittler was also the first Maple Leaf ever to hit one hundred points in a season, achieving that plateau in 1975–76; he then did it again in 1977–78, when he got 117.

DID YOU KNOW ...
that the last time a Toronto Maple Leaf won the
NHL's scoring title was way back in 1937–38, when
Gord Drillon did it with fifty-two points?

What Canadian holds the record for the most goals in a single NHL season by a defenceman?

You might say Bobby Orr, but you would be wrong. The Edmonton Oilers' Paul Coffey potted forty-eight goals in 1985–86 to achieve the most goals by a defenceman in a single season. He also holds the record for most goals — twelve in 1985 — by a defenceman in a single playoff year. Coffey was a member of the amazing 1980s Edmonton Oilers and won three Stanley Cups with them. The year he achieved the most goals by a defenceman in a season, Coffey racked up 138 points, his career best and one short of Orr's still-standing record for a defender. Despite all that offensive power, Coffey was traded to the Pittsburgh Penguins in 1987 by owner Peter Pocklington, one of that man's many boneheaded deals. Coffey continued to play superbly for the Penguins, reaching 113 points in 1988–89 and eventually winning another Stanley Cup with his new club in 1991. After that Coffey bopped around the league, playing in Los Angeles, Detroit, Hartford, Philadelphia, Chicago, Carolina, and Boston, where he retired during the 2000–01 season (he has the lesser distinction of having played on the most teams of any one-thousand-career-point player). During his career Coffey won the Norris Trophy as best defenceman three times (1985, 1986, and 1995). Incidentally, Raymond Bourque, who played most of his career with the Boston Bruins and retired with the Colorado Avalanche, has the most career goals (410), assists (1,169), and points (1,579) accumulated by a defenceman.

What Canadian NHL player holds the record for the most fifty-goal seasons?

Even when single-season scoring tallies started escalating after NHL expansion in 1967–68, scoring fifty goals in a single season still meant something as a personal plateau, and it continues to. The Montreal Canadiens' Maurice "Rocket" Richard was the first to do it in 1944–45, and achieved it in fifty games. Teammate Bernard "Boom Boom" Geoffrion was the second to hit the mark in 1960–61. The first player to pot more than fifty was the Chicago Black Hawks' Bobby Hull, who got fifty-four in 1965–66 (Hull had earlier joined the fifty-goal club in 1961–62). As to who's recorded the most fifty-goal seasons in a career, that's a tie between Mike Bossy and Wayne Gretzky. Both did it nine times. However, Bossy only played ten seasons in his career (all with the New York Islanders), while the Great One got his nine in twenty seasons with the Edmonton Oilers, Los Angeles Kings, St. Louis Blues, and New York Rangers. What's more, Bossy nabbed his nine in consecutive seasons from 1977–78 to 1985–86, which is also a record, one he doesn't share with anybody.

Which Canadian was the first NHL player to score one hundred points in a regular season?

The Detroit Red Wings' Gordie Howe almost hit one hundred points in 1952–53, when he got ninety-five, but it took more than another decade and a half before the Boston Bruins' Phil Esposito broke the one hundred barrier in 1968–69 on his way to ending up with 126 points. Of course, Wayne Gretzky blew everybody away with his remarkable feats in the 1980s, topping two hundred points four times, with a record 215 in 1985–86. The Great One is still the only NHL player to score more than two hundred points in one season. The Pittsburgh Penguins' Mario Lemieux came close in 1988–89, when he managed 199 points. Incidentally, Number 99 has the most one hundred-point seasons (fifteen) and the most consecutive one hundred-pointers (thirteen).

Which Canadian player was the first to score more than five hundred NHL goals in his career?

Few players dominated his era the way Maurice "Rocket" Richard dominated his. On October 19, 1957, at the Montreal Forum, he scaled another plateau when he scored goal number five hundred, the first player to do so in the NHL. The Rocket was playing in his 863rd game. Strangely enough, Richard never won a scoring championship. In fact, he holds the record for being the runner-up, accomplishing that unfortunate mark five times in 1945, 1947, 1951, 1954, and 1955. To date only two NHL players have scored more than eight hundred regular-season career goals: Wayne Gretzky (894) and Gordie Howe (801).

DID YOU KNOW ...
that Gordie Howe was forty-one and in his twenty-third year with the Detroit Red Wings in 1968–69, when he achieved his only one-hundred-point season? Howe is the sole forty-one-year-old in the NHL to ever achieve this plateau.

Which Canadian player is the only rookie to win the NHL scoring championship?

Scrappy, surly Nels Stewart was already twenty-three when he joined the NHL as a Montreal Maroon in 1925–26. Previously, "Old Poison," as he was nicknamed, had played for five years with the Cleveland Indians in the USA Hockey Association. Born in Montreal, Stewart scored thirty-four goals and eight assists for forty-two points in thirty-six games in his inaugural season. That year he also won the Hart Trophy as most valuable player and helped the Maroons to win the Stanley Cup. Old Poison won a second Hart in 1929–30 and scored thirty-nine goals and sixteen assists for fifty-five points in only forty-four games. The next season, on January 3, 1931, he potted two goals in four seconds, an NHL record that still stands, though it was equalled by the Winnipeg Jets' Deron Quint in 1995. The record for most goals scored by a rookie in the NHL belongs to Teemu Selanne, who got seventy-six in 1992–93 while playing for the Winnipeg Jets. That same year Selanne racked up 132 points, which is also a record for a rookie.

DID YOU KNOW ...
that Sidney Crosby is the youngest NHL player and the only teenager ever to win the Art Ross Trophy as scoring champion? He achieved that in his second season in 2006–07 with the Pittsburgh Penguins, when he scored thirty-six goals and eighty-four assists for 120 points.

Which Canadian goaltender has won the most NHL regular-season games?

Montreal-native Martin Brodeur, over his twenty-one NHL seasons with the New Jersey Devils (and a brief stint with the St. Louis Blues in his last season), notched an incredible 691 victories. It's a record that's not likely to be toppled anytime soon. Over his long career he picked up four Vezina Trophies as best goaltender in the league, in 2003, 2004, 2007, and 2008.

Which Canadian goalie has the most playoff victories?

That would be Patrick Roy, with 151 career playoff victories with the Montreal Canadiens and the Colorado Avalanche. What's more, he's the only player to ever win the Conn Smythe Trophy three times as the most valuable player in the Stanley Cup playoffs. He won the award in 1986, 1993, and 2001.

What Canadian goalie has recorded the most regular-season shutouts in the NHL?

For many years that distinction belonged to the mercurial Terry Sawchuk, who accumulated 103 shutouts in twenty-one seasons playing for the Red Wings, Bruins, Maple Leafs, Kings, and Rangers between 1949 and 1970. His record held up for forty years until it was broken in 2009–10 by the New Jersey Devils' star netminder Martin Brodeur. Brodeur, who hails from Montreal, ended his career with a grand total of 125 regular-season shutouts over his twenty-one NHL seasons.

Which Canadian was the first goaltender in the NHL to wear a mask?

It's hard to believe now, but for decades hockey goalies didn't wear masks. After he broke his cheekbone, Clint Benedict of the Montreal Maroons donned a makeshift leather mask for a couple of games in January 1930, making him the first NHL netminder to wear face protection. But Benedict felt that the contraption obscured his vision on low shots, so he discarded it. The first NHL goalie to wear a mask regularly, of course, was the Montreal Canadiens' Jacques Plante, who put on a homemade fibreglass job during a 3–1 Habs victory over the New York Rangers on November 1, 1959.

Which Canadian NHL player was the first to wear a helmet?

As with goalies playing without masks, forwards or defencemen playing without helmets for decade upon decade is hard to believe now. Helmets started to become more common in the 1970s, but the first NHL player to don one was George Owen of the Boston Bruins, who debuted with the club on January 10, 1929. The Hamilton, Ontario–born Owen had played football at university and reportedly wore his leather football helmet as a rookie defenceman. Owen and the Bruins went on to win the Stanley Cup in 1929.

Which Canadian NHL player was the last to play without a helmet?

The days of seeing an NHL player's hair or lack of it on the ice started to be numbered in the 1970s, especially after the league made it mandatory in 1979 for all players entering the NHL to don one. Anyone already in the league at that time could still go helmetless if they so desired. London,

Ontario, native, centreman Craig MacTavish, once an integral part of the Edmonton Oilers in the late 1980s and the early 1990s, continued to display his greying locks until his final game with the St. Louis Blues during the 1997 Stanley Cup playoffs.

Which Canadian was the first black player to see ice time in the NHL?

Black players and managers have been noticeably absent from the NHL for much of its existence. Whether this had more to do with the fact that almost all big-league players before 1970 hailed from Canada and in those days the country had, relatively speaking, a small black population, or with the fact that there was an active colour barrier in place, is open to debate. But one thing isn't subject to conjecture: Fredericton, New Brunswick–born Willie O'Ree was the first player of African descent to play in the NHL. The right winger's stint in the major league was brief — he played two games for the Boston Bruins in January 1958 and forty-three matches for the same team in 1960–61 — but his place in hockey history is significant. The New Brunswicker experienced much racial abuse at the hands of opposing players, as well as fans, the latter insulting him by throwing black hats on to the ice. O'Ree may not have had a lengthy career in the NHL and only recorded fourteen points in the big league, but he was a legend in the minors, playing in various leagues such as the American Hockey League and the Western Hockey League (largely for the San Diego Gulls) well into the 1970s. He did all this even though he was legally blind in one eye, due to an errant puck during a game when he was eighteen.

Who was the first full-blooded aboriginal player in the NHL?

A Saskatchewan Cree named Fred Sasakamoose from the Sandy Lake Reserve appeared in eleven games with the Chicago Black Hawks in 1953–54, making him the first full-blooded aboriginal player to make it to the NHL. Sasakamoose recorded no points and notched six penalty minutes in his short NHL dalliance. Later, though, he was the playing coach of the Kamloops Chiefs. During his time in British Columbia, the Shuswap and Chilcotin Bands of the province's interior awarded him the name Chief Thunder Stick, a title he assumed when he was elected chief of the Sandy Lake Cree.

What kind of car was Tim Horton driving when he was killed?

Cochrane, Ontario–born Tim Horton is now better known as the franchise name of a colossal doughnut-and-coffee empire, but for twenty-four seasons he was one of the NHL's most durable, dependable defencemen. After a couple of brief stints with the Toronto Maple Leafs in the late 1940s and early 1950s, Horton came to stay in 1952–53. He was a fixture on the Leafs' defence until he was traded to the New York Rangers in 1969–70. During the 1960s he and a crackerjack blue-line squad that included Allan Stanley, Bob Baun, and Carl Brewer helped Toronto win four Stanley Cups (1962–64, 1967). Horton's sixteen points in thirteen playoff games in 1962 set a record for defencemen (long since surpassed), and he was capable of rushing up the ice in a burst of speed to deliver a pretty hard slap shot to an opponent's net. The brawny defender played briefly for the Pittsburgh Penguins after his time with the Rangers, then ended up with the Buffalo Sabres and back with his old Leafs' coach George "Punch" Imlach in 1972–73. Horton, then in his forties, wanted to retire the next season, but Imlach persuaded him otherwise. On February 21, 1974, Horton was killed in a car accident near St. Catharines, Ontario, after a game in Toronto. A notorious speeder, he was headed back to Buffalo in the new Ford Pantera sports car that Imlach had given him as a signing bonus to play one last season. During his long NHL career, he played 1,446 regular-season games and scored 115 goals and 403 assists for 518 points, adding another eleven goals and thirty-nine assists in the playoffs. Today the doughnut company Horton founded in Hamilton, Ontario, in 1964 (later taking on former Hamilton, Ontario, policeman Ron Joyce as partner) has nothing to do with his survivors except in name, but it has mushroomed into a billion-dollar corporation that employs more than one hundred thousand people and has 4,492 restaurants in nine countries (2016).

What NHL superstar was offered the position of governor general of Canada?

After Jean Béliveau retired from the front office of the Montreal Canadiens in 1993, he was offered the post of governor general the next year. However, he declined the honour, citing family obligations. Although he never idolized the way his Canadiens teammate Maurice Richard was, Béliveau was one of the greatest hockey players ever to lace on a pair of skates. Born in Trois-Rivières, Quebec, the gentlemanly centre played twenty seasons (eighteen full) for the Canadiens and scored 507 goals and 712 assists for 1,219 points. In the Stanley Cup playoffs he added another seventy-nine goals and ninety-seven assists in seventeen competitions, helping the Habs win ten Stanley Cups. Béliveau won the Art Ross Trophy in 1956, the Conn Smythe Trophy in 1965, and the Hart Trophy in 1956 and 1964. "Le Gros Bill," as he was nicknamed, retired as a player in 1971 and was employed by Montreal as vice-president of corporate affairs for twenty-two years. Béliveau passed away in 2014.

? DID YOU KNOW ...
that the first NHL shutout was recorded by the
Montreal Canadiens' great goaltender Georges
Vézina? Appropriately, given the teams' latter-day
rivalry, he achieved this milestone on February
18, 1918, in a game against the Toronto Arenas
(later the St. Patricks, then the Maple Leafs). Vézina
and the Habs won the match 9–0 in the league's
twenty-ninth game in its first season.

When and where in Canada was the first official NHL All-Star Game played?

Great hockey isn't something usually associated with an NHL All-Star Game, but fans do get to see the year's best players assembled in one spot, the players selected get to have a bit of fun (and grab some more money), and players who aren't picked get a rest. The league began choosing All-Star teams in 1930–31 and staged a few All-Star benefit games for the survivors of dead players (Ace Bailey in 1933, Howie Morenz in 1937, and Babe Siebert in 1939). However, the first official All-Star Game was played on October 13, 1947, at Maple Leaf Gardens. The initial format had the Stanley Cup champions from the previous season play a team of All-Stars picked from the league's other five clubs. In 1947 the All-Stars beat the Stanley Cup–winning Toronto Maple Leafs 4–3. Since that first official match, the All-Star Game has been moved from the beginning of the season to the middle, and now the Eastern Conference All-Stars play the Western Conference All-Stars.

What led to the Richard riots in Montreal?

In a game between the Boston Bruins and the Montreal Canadiens in Boston on March 13, 1955, Maurice "Rocket" Richard was cut in the head by the Bruins' Hal Laycoe with a high stick. The wound eventually required five stitches, and Laycoe was later assessed five-minute and ten-minute penalties, but the game's action continued because the Habs had the puck. As soon as the whistle blew, Richard skated over to Laycoe and struck the Bruin over the head and shoulders with his stick. Laycoe dropped his gloves and urged the Rocket to fight with his fists, but a linesman, Cliff Thompson, grabbed Richard from behind and took his stick away. Richard broke away and was able to strike Laycoe a few more times with loose sticks, then attacked Thompson, too. After he was finally subdued and sent to the dressing room for repairs, Richard was officially thrown out of the game and fined one hundred dollars. But it didn't stop there. Hitting an official was a serious offence, and after a hearing NHL president Clarence Campbell decided to suspend the Habs' superstar for the rest of the season and for the entire playoffs, at the time the longest suspension in the league's history for an on-ice infraction. The decision hit the city of Montreal, and the entire province of Quebec, like a ton of pucks. People cried, a bus driver nearly hit a train when he heard the news, the town seethed. Without Richard the Canadiens' chances in the postseason were somewhat reduced, plus the Rocket's close race for the scoring lead was stymied. So, on St. Patrick's Day, March 17, when the Canadiens, without Richard, took on the Detroit Red Wings in Montreal, there was danger in the air. The Wings were battling the Habs for first place in the league, and the Wings' general manager, Jack Adams, had supported Campbell unquestioningly concerning Richard's sentence. Worse, Campbell himself attended the game at the Forum (and so did Richard), a fact that made thousands of fans inside and outside the arena see red. Not surprisingly, the game was never finished and was forfeited to the Wings. A tear-gas bomb went off, all hell broke loose, and before the long night was over, the Forum was trashed, fifteen blocks of stores and shops around the rink were looted and damaged, numerous cars were savaged, and twelve policemen and twenty-five civilians were injured, not to mention the dozens of people who were arrested. It was the worst riot in sports history, and still is. Was there something more to the affair than just anger over Richard's suspension? Did the violence have something to do with simmering French-Canadian nationalism and anti-English frustration? No one can really say for sure, but what is known is that Quebec's Quiet Revolution was just around the corner in the 1960s, and the province would soon change irrevocably. What's also certain is that Detroit finished first in 1954–55; the Habs and the Wings faced each other in the Stanley Cup Finals and the latter took the cup; and Maurice Richard lost out to his own teammate, Bernard "Boom Boom" Geoffrion, in the scoring race (Boom Boom was even booed by Canadiens fans). The Rocket never did win an Art Ross Trophy. The year of the riot was probably his best shot at it.

What actually killed Howie Morenz, the Montreal Canadiens' first superstar?

Not too many hockey players become part of hockey lore in a way that takes them beyond the mere living and enshrouds them in myth. Mitchell, Ontario–born Howarth "Howie" Morenz is one of those select people. At five foot nine and seventy-five kilograms he was quite small for a hockey player, even in his day, but almost no one was as fast or as skilled. Long before Guy Lafleur, Jean Béliveau, and Maurice Richard, Morenz was the Montreal Canadiens' first true superstar scoring machine. The whirling dervish centre won scoring championships in 1928 and 1931; copped the Hart Trophy as most valuable player in 1928, 1931, and 1932; and won Stanley Cups with the Habs in 1924, 1930, and 1931. After electrifying fans everywhere, especially in the new NHL markets of New York, Detroit, Boston, and Chicago, with his exciting speed and deadly accuracy as a goal scorer in the 1920s and early 1930s, Morenz was hit by a spate of injuries, and his impact on the ice diminished so much that even hometown fans began to boo him. In 1934 he was finally traded to the Chicago Black

Hawks, who eventually dealt him to the New York Rangers. In 1936–37 the Canadiens, now in the doldrums both at the gate and in their game, reacquired their ace, who scored four goals and sixteen assists for the team before a terrible accident occurred on January 28, 1937, in a game against the Chicago Black Hawks in the Montreal Forum. At one fateful point in the first period, Morenz barrelled into the corner after the puck. When he smashed into the boards, one of his skates got caught in a crack in the ice just as Black Hawks' defenceman Earl Siebert crashed into him from behind. The Mitchell Meteor's body went one way while his leg remained locked between the ice and the boards. The Habs fans were deathly silent as the snap from Morenz's bones reverberated throughout the rink. In the hospital the man dubbed the "Babe Ruth of Hockey" was told by the doctors that he would never again play the game he loved. Morenz sank into a profound depression. On March 8, after more than a month in the hospital, he decided to leave despite the cast on his leg. He took one step, dropped to the floor, and died. The cause was put down to a coronary embolism, though more sentimental types suggested Morenz's heart just burst with despair. He was only thirty-four. Morenz's funeral was the kind given to revered movie stars like Rudolph Valentino. Fifteen thousand mourners crammed into the Forum on March 11, while another fifty thousand thronged the streets outside the rink. Interestingly enough, the final game at the Forum was played on March 11, 1996, exactly fifty-nine years after the Canadien Comet's funeral.

Where in Canada was the first NHL game played outdoors?

Outdoor NHL games have been a big hit with the fans, the media, and the players lately. The first regular-season match held outdoors was dubbed the "Heritage Classic" and took place on November 22, 2003, in Edmonton. It pitted the Edmonton Oilers against the Montreal Canadiens. More than fifty-seven thousand spectators braved bone-chilling -18°C temperatures to watch the Habs edge the Oilers 4–3.

What Canadian Hall of Fame hockey player only had one eye?

Few hockey players have had such a brief career and made such a lasting impact. Ottawa-born Frank McGee, known as "One-Eye" after he lost an orb to an errant puck in 1900, was the nephew of Thomas D'Arcy McGee, who was one of Canada's Fathers of Confederation and met his end at the hands of an assassin in 1868. Only five foot six and 63.5 kilograms, McGee made up for his diminutive size with pinpoint scoring and crafty stick-handling. As a youth the high-scoring forward played centre and rover (a seventh position now eliminated) for various teams in the country's capital, then graduated to the fabled Ottawa Silver Seven in 1902, helping the team win its first Stanley Cup in 1903. For the next three years Ottawa successfully defended its title to the cup ten times before losing the hardware to the Montreal Wanderers in 1906. McGee's most famous exploit was the scoring of fourteen goals in one game on January 16, 1905, against a Stanley Cup challenger from Dawson City, Yukon — still the best anyone has done in a cup match. The Silver Seven won that match 23–2. In 1904–05 McGee scored seventeen goals in six games and tied Jack Marshall for the Federal Amateur Hockey League scoring title. The next season, playing in the Eastern Canada Amateur Hockey Association, he did even better, getting twenty-eight goals in a mere seven games, but still finished third in the scoring race in that league. McGee scored seventy-one goals in twenty-three regular-season games in his four years with Ottawa, with another sixty-three goals in twenty-two playoff matches. He was only twenty-four in 1907, when after sustaining many serious injuries in a particularly violent era in hockey, he decided to retire to take a federal government job. Despite his damaged eye, McGee went to France as an army officer to fight for Canada in the First World War. He was killed at the Battle of the Somme in 1916.

What incredible feat did Mario Lemieux accomplish on New Year's Eve 1988?

During his career, the Pittsburgh Penguins' Mario Lemieux accomplished incredible feats and provided hockey fans with some of the game's most memorable moments, but on December 31, 1988, he did something pretty extraordinary, even for him. In a game against the New Jersey Devils the Magnificent One became the first and thus far only NHL player to score goals in five different ways. Lemieux put the puck into the Devils' net at even strength, on the power play, short-handed, on a penalty shot, and into an empty net in an 8–6 Penguins victory.

DID YOU KNOW ...

that at 3:00 p.m. on October 13, 1951, the Chicago Black Hawks and the Toronto Maple Leafs staged a one-period exhibition match at Maple Leaf Gardens especially for Princess Elizabeth (the future Queen Elizabeth II) and the Duke of Edinburgh? It was Elizabeth's first attendance at a professional hockey match. Later that day, without royalty on hand, the two teams hit the ice for their season opener, which the Black Hawks won 3-1. Decades later, on October 6, 2002, Elizabeth II became the first queen to drop a puck in a faceoff at a hockey match when she visited Canada during her Golden Jubilee. The occasion was a pre-season game between the Vancouver Canucks and the San Jose Sharks in Vancouver. After she did her ceremonial duty, Queen Elizabeth spent the first period watching the game in a private box with Wayne Gretzky.

Which unlikely opponent beat Canada's hockey team in the gold-medal match at the 1936 Winter Olympic Games?

After winning gold in hockey without breaking a sweat at the 1920, 1924, 1928, and 1932 Olympics, Canada finally encountered some competition at the 1936 Winter Olympic Games in Garmisch-Partenkirchen, Germany, as storm clouds of future war were already beginning to gather, and the Nazis used both the Winter and Summer Olympic Games as a showcase for their delusions of Aryan superiority. Represented by the Port Arthur Bearcats, Canada easily vanquished its opponents in the first round, but in the semifinals the Bearcats came up against a Great Britain team stocked with a number of men who held British passports but who lived and played hockey in Canada. The Bearcats lost 2–1 to the British, who didn't lose any hockey matches during the games (though they did tie 0–0 with the United States). Britain won the gold medal, while Canada had to settle for the silver, and the United States got bronze. There would not be another Olympics until 1948.

Which Canadian scored the first goal and assisted on the last goal of the 1972 Canada-Soviet Union Summit Series?

The most important single tournament in the history of hockey was an eight-game series played in September 1972 between a team of Canada's National Hockey League professionals and the Soviet Union's national team. The event ushered in the modern era of international hockey, the breakdown of all professional-amateur barriers, and the emergence of the multicultural makeup of the NHL. The series evolved out of Canada's withdrawal from international competition and the Soviets' desire to play best against best, with four games in Canada (Montreal, Toronto, Winnipeg, Vancouver) and four games in the Soviet Union (all in Moscow). Thirty seconds into the first match in Montreal, the Boston Bruins' Phil Esposito scored the very first goal in the series, and the Canadians sat back, figuring the tournament would be a cakewalk. However, the Soviets stormed back in the game and embarrassed Canada by whipping them 7–3. Things improved marginally in the second match in Toronto, when Canada fought back and won 2–1. After that Canadian nerves began to fray when the Soviets tied Canada 4–4 in Winnipeg and clobbered their hosts 5–3 in Vancouver. The West Coast fans booed Team Canada as it skated off the ice when the game was finished, and an emotional Esposito pleaded for respect on national television. After two violent exhibition games in Sweden to adapt to the larger ice surface, Canada entered the Soviet Union in a desperate situation, especially after the team lost the fifth game 5–4 in Moscow. As it turned out, and as every Canadian now knows, Canada went on to win the next three games 3–2, 4–3, and 6–5. The winning goal in all three matches was scored by Paul Henderson. That final game was watched by more people in Canada — something like sixteen million — than any other televised show before or since. Certainly, the country as a whole breathed a collective sigh of relief at the final tally: four wins for Canada, three losses, and one tie. As to who assisted Paul Henderson on that last score against the Soviets' netminder Vladislav Tretiak, the goal heard across Canada if not the world, it was Phil Esposito. "Espo" also ended up being the scoring leader for the series, with seven goals and six assists.

D I D   Y O U   K N O W ...

that Phil Esposito, who displayed an aggressive, almost xenophobic dislike of Soviet players during the 1972 Canada-Soviet Union Summit Series, walked his daughter, Connie, down the aisle in 1996 as she married a Russian hockey player named Alexander Selivanov? At the time Selivanov was a member of the NHL's Tampa Bay Lightning, and Esposito was president and general manager for the team.

Who were the first three Canadians to join the "Triple Gold Club"?

Prior to the Winter Olympic Games in Salt Lake City in 2002, only ten people had won a Stanley Cup, as well as Olympic gold and a World Championship in hockey, and all of them were European. That year, though, Canada won its first gold medal in hockey since 1952. On the Canadian team were Joe Sakic, Rob Blake, and Brendan Shanahan, all of whom had previously won Stanley Cups and World Championships. Now they, too, were part of the rarefied so-called "Triple Gold Club."

As of January 1, 2017, there are twenty-seven players who have accomplished the feat — ten Canadians, nine Swedes, six Russians, and two Czechs. In addition to those first three, the other Canadians who have accomplished it are: Scott Niedermayer (2004), Chris Pronger (2007), Eric Staal and Jonathan Toews (2010), Patrice Bergeron (2011), Sidney Crosby (2015), and Corey Perry (2016).

What did Canadian Abigail Hoffman do that caused an international furor?

In 1956, at the age of nine, Abigail "Abby" Hoffman cut her hair and joined a boys' hockey team as Ab Hoffman. The plucky girl's team did so well that it made the playoffs, and players were required to produce their birth certificates. After it was discovered that Ab was a girl, the league and the country went ballistic. In fact, the news caught the attention of a good deal of the world's media at the time. Even though her team had no problem with her, Hoffman bowed out of organized hockey after the club lost. Eventually, she turned her attention to track and field and went on to compete in four Summer Olympic Games — in 1964, 1968, 1972, and 1976. At the last, the first held in Canada (Montreal), she was the country's flag-bearer. Hoffman won the gold medal twice in the 880-yard event at the 1963 and 1966 Commonwealth Games, and she also struck gold in the 800-metre race at the 1971 Pan American Games, not to mention winning bronze medals at the same competition in 1967 and 1975 in the 800-metre and 1,500-metre races.

When was the first Women's World Hockey Championship held?

Informally begun in 1987 in Toronto as an invitational tournament, the Women's World Hockey Championship has become the pre-eminent event in women's hockey, with the exception of the Winter Olympic Games. Not surprisingly, Canada won that first event. At the first six championships (1990, 1992, 1994, 1997, 1999, 2000), under the auspices of the International Ice Hockey Federation, the results were the same: Canada gold, the United States silver, Finland bronze. In 2001 Canada and the United States once again took gold and silver, respectively, but Russia nabbed bronze. The 2003 championship was cancelled due to the outbreak of SARS, and since then Canada has won gold three times (2004, 2007, and 2012), and the United States has struck gold seven times (2005, 2008, 2009, 2011, 2013, 2015, and 2016). As of 2016 the totals look like this: Canada ten, United States seven. The tournament isn't held in years when there's a Winter Olympic Games.

Which Canadian was the first woman to play in the NHL?

Arguably the most famous female hockey player in the world in the early 1990s, Manon Rhéaume, born in Lac Beauport, Quebec, was the first woman to suit up with a National Hockey League team when she played goal in a 1992 pre-season match for the Tampa Bay Lightning against the St. Louis Blues. The next year she played another exhibition game for the Lightning against the Boston Bruins. After that she tended goal for a number of men's minor-league clubs. In 1992 Rhéaume made her first appearance with Canada's national team, and she helped it win gold medals at the

Women's World Championship in 1992 and 1994. Prior to the 1997 World Championship, she was cut from Team Canada, but she made a comeback at the 1998 Winter Olympic Games in Nagano, Japan. She played well, but Canada lost the gold to the U.S. team and had to settle for silver. Rhéaume announced her retirement from hockey in summer 2000.

SIX TOP CANADIAN WOMEN'S HOCKEY PLAYERS

- Hayley Wickenheiser: Gold medals at the 2002, 2006, 2010, and 2014 Winter Olympic Games. Gold medals at the Women's World Hockey Championship in 1994, 1997, 1999, 2000, 2001, 2003, and 2007.
- Angela James: Gold medals at the Women's World Hockey Championship in 1990, 1992, 1994, and 1997.
- Cassie Campbell: Gold medals at the 2002 and 2006 Winter Olympic Games. Gold medals at the Women's World Hockey Championship in 1994, 1997, 1999, 2000, 2001, and 2004.
- Danielle Goyette: Gold medals at the 2002 and 2006 Winter Olympic Games. Gold medals at the Women's World Hockey Championship in 1992, 1994, 1997, 1999, 2000, 2001, 2004, and 2007.
- Geraldine Heaney: Gold medal at the 2002 Winter Olympic Games. Gold medals at the Women's World Hockey Championship in 1992, 1994, 1997, 1999, 2000, and 2001.
- Jayna Hefford: Second all-time in Team Canada history in games played (267), goals (157), and points (291). Four-time Olympic gold medallist, 2002, 2006, 2010, and 2014 (silver in 1998). Seven-time world champion (1997, 1999, 2000, 2001, 2004, 2007, and 2012) and five-time silver medallist (2005, 2008, 2009, 2011, and 2013) at the World Championships. A twelve-time gold medallist at the 3 Nations/4 Nations Cup, winning five silver medals there, as well.

DID YOU KNOW ...

that in 2002 Jayna Hefford famously scored the game-winning goal with two seconds remaining in Canada's victory against the United States in Salt Lake City?

THE
BEAUTIFUL
GAME ... NOW
IN CANADA

What is the Voyageurs Cup?

The Voyageurs Cup is the only trophy for top-level professional soccer in Canada. From 2002 to 2007 the cup was awarded annually to the Canadian United Soccer League (USL) division team finishing with the best record from regular season matches against other Canadian teams in the USL. Since 2008 the trophy has been awarded to the winner of the Canadian Championship. Montreal Impact has won the cup a whopping nine times as of 2016.

DID YOU KNOW ...

that the Inuit played a game called *asqaqtuk*, which involved booting a heavy ball stuffed with grass, caribou hair, and moss across the Arctic tundra between goalposts which were as much as sixteen kilometres apart?

Has Canada ever won a major international soccer tournament?

The answer is yes! Five times, actually. The first time for the men's squad was at the 1904 Summer Olympic Games in St. Louis. Canada sent Galt FC as its representative team, and Galt defeated the only two other teams (both American) entered without being scored on. The contest is considered to be official by the IOC, but not by FIFA. The second instance was more challenging, as Canada competed in a field of nine national teams from the Confederation of North, Central American, and Caribbean Association Football to win the 1985 CONCACAF

Championship. Then in 2000 Canada emerged victorious from a field of eight teams to take the CONCACAF Gold Cup. The Canadian women's team is also two-time CONCACAF Women's Gold Cup champions, with victories in 1998 and 2010.

?

DID YOU KNOW ...
that the first international soccer game played without involving a British side was between the United States and Canada? The game was played in Newark, New Jersey, on November 28, 1885. The Canadians won by a score of 1-0.

What two records did Canadian Kara Lang set when she was just fifteen years old?

Kara Lang holds the women's football world record for the youngest Canadian player to score a full international goal. She scored against Wales at the Algarve Cup on March 3, 2002, at age fifteen years, 132 days. She must have been on a roll, because her senior debut, two days earlier, had been a Canadian record for youngest senior women's cap. Lang was inducted into the Canadian Soccer Hall of Fame as a player in 2015.

What was the first Canadian Major League Soccer team?

That would be Toronto FC, which was formed in 2006 and plays at BMO Field on the grounds of the Canadian National Exhibition. The team set an MLS record in season ticket sales, selling fourteen thousand before it had even appeared in a game. As of 2016 Canada has three teams in MLS — Toronto FC, Vancouver Whitecaps, and Montreal Impact.

Which Canadian soccer player has scored the most international goals?

With 250 games under her belt (as of January 1, 2017), Burnaby, British Columbia, native Christine Sinclair is Canada's top scorer when it comes to international competition. After fifteen years with Canadian national teams, she has scored 165 goals for her country. Sinclair has played in four Women's World Cups and three Summer Olympic Games (2008, 2012, and 2016), and in 2012 she was voted Canadian athlete of the year and female athlete of the year. She was inducted into Canada's Walk of Fame in 2013. Worldwide, she is second in all-time international goals after retired American player Abby Wambach, who has 184.

SCOOPS ON CANADIAN HOOPS

Which Canadian
invented basketball?

James Naismith, from Bennies Corners in Ontario's Ottawa Valley, became interested in sports when he was a theological student at McGill University. His favourite game was football, and his fellow ministers-in-training would pray for his soul because they considered football to be a tool of the devil. In 1891, as a physical education instructor at the YMCA school in Springfield, Massachusetts, Naismith realized that his students found the regimen of indoor calisthenics and exercises boring. He decided to invent a new indoor game that would be easy to learn and fun to play. After some failed experiments with football, soccer, and lacrosse, Naismith came up with basketball. When he could not find square boxes to use as targets, he used a pair of half-bushel peach baskets. In the first basketball game ever played, a man on a ladder had to retrieve the ball every time a basket was scored.

What Canadian team lost
the first NBA game?

The first NBA game was played on November 1, 1946, in Toronto. The New York Knicks defeated the Toronto Huskies 68–66. The Huskies folded the next year.

Why did Toronto Raptors fans wear baby bibs printed with the number 15 on April 15, 2005?

On April 15, 2005, Toronto fans at a home game showed their scorn for former Raptor Vince Carter, who wears number 15, by donning baby bibs with his number printed on them. It was the first time Carter had returned to Toronto after being traded to the New Jersey Nets. Carter, once a superstar in Toronto, fell out of favour with fans after suffering chronic injuries and then making it clear through the poor quality of his play that he wanted a trade. By wearing the bibs, Toronto fans were calling him a big baby.

Who was the first Canadian to be selected first overall in an NBA draft?

In 2013 the Cleveland Cavaliers picked Brampton, Ontario's Anthony Bennett as first overall in the NBA draft. The next year Andrew Wiggins of Vaughan, Ontario, was the first overall pick, going to the Cleveland Cavaliers, making Canada the first country, other than the Unites States, to have back-to-back number one draft picks in the league. Wiggins was named NBA Rookie of the Year for the 2014–15 season, and he currently plays for the Minnesota Timberwolves (2014–present).

Who is the most successful Canadian to ever play in the NBA?

That honour goes to the incredibly talented Steve Nash. In his nineteen-year career as a player with the Phoenix Suns, Dallas Mavericks, and Los Angeles Lakers, Nash was named the NBA's Most Valuable Player twice (2005, 2006), is an eight-time All-Star (2002, 2003, 2005–08, 2010, 2012) and five-time assists leader (2005–07, 2010–11), and had four 50–40–90 seasons (shooting percentage at or above 50 percent for field goals, 40 percent for three-pointers, and 90 percent for free throws), more than any other player in NBA history. The Canadian point guard's jersey, number 13, was retired by the Phoenix Suns, and he was also a recipient of the J. Walter Kennedy Citizenship Award, given for "outstanding service and dedication to the community" (2007).

CANADA'S OTHER NATIONAL GAME

What is *baaga'adowe*?

Baaga'adowe is the Ojibwa word for the game more widely known as lacrosse. The early French settlers saw the aboriginal people playing the game, and they named it for the sticks they used to toss the ball. The aboriginal way of playing lacrosse was a wild, no-holds-barred melee that could involve as many as five hundred men on each team, and often resulted in broken bones and even death. In 1867 William George Beers of Montreal formed the National Lacrosse Association of Canada, which promoted a set of rules by which the game was to be played. There is no record that lacrosse was ever made Canada's official national game. Beers also made such activities as snowshoeing and tobogganing popular recreational activities.

Who invented lacrosse?

The game that eventually came to be called lacrosse was created by aboriginal people before European settlers arrived in North America. Its name was *dehuntshigwa'es* in Onondaga ("men hit a rounded object"), *da-nah-wah'uwsdi* in Eastern Cherokee ("little war"), *tewaarathon* in Mohawk language ("little brother of war"), and *baaga'adowe* in Ojibwa ("bump hips"). These games, played on large open plains, could last several days with as many as one hundred to one thousand men from opposing villages or tribes taking part.

Why is lacrosse called *lacrosse*?

Lacrosse was considered good training for aboriginal warriors. Teams consisting of hundreds of players often involved entire villages in brutal contests that could last as long as three days. To the French explorers who were the first Europeans to see the game, the stick resembled a bishop's ceremonial staff, called a crozier, surmounted by a cross, or *la crosse* — and the sport had a new name.

?

D I D   Y O U   K N O W ...
that lacrosse is Canada's official national sport of summer, while Canada's official national sport of winter is ice hockey?

What were early lacrosse sticks and balls made of?

Aboriginal people used three types of lacrosse sticks. Communities such as Cherokee, Choctaw, and Seminole in the southeastern United States played a version called *toli* that used two sticks per player, each measuring around sixty centimetres long. One stick was held in each hand, and the player cupped a ball of stuffed deer hide between small, netted hoops on the ends of the two sticks. In the Great Lakes region, bands such as the Ojibwa, Winnebago, and Menominee used only one stick per player, which measured about ninety centimetres long. A round, netted pocket measuring 7–10 centimetres in diameter on the end of the stick was used to carry a wooden ball. Meanwhile, in the northeast, the Iroquois and others used the sticks that became the model for contemporary equipment, which were typically longer than ninety centimetres. Curved into a hook at one end, they were strung with netting inside the hook and down the shaft of the stick. Balls were made of deer hide stuffed with hair.

DID YOU KNOW ...
that the aboriginal people of the Great Lakes used the extremely dense wood from tree knots to make lacrosse balls?

What is a modern lacrosse ball made of?

The modern lacrosse ball is made of solid rubber. It is typically white or yellow. It is usually between nineteen and twenty centimetres in circumference, about 6.5 centimetres in diameter, and weighs between 140 and 150 grams.

DID YOU KNOW ...
that although lacrosse is North America's oldest sport, it was not until August 2008 that an international body — called the Federation of International Lacrosse — was organized to oversee the sport worldwide?

DID YOU KNOW ...
that on June 2, 1763, the Ottawa Chief Pontiac
invited the British garrison of Fort Michilimackinac to
watch a game of *baaga'adowe* outside the walls of
the fort? While the soldiers watched, with the gates
of the stockade wide open, the teams gradually
worked their way closer to the fort. Suddenly, the
ball was tossed over the wall. This was the signal to
attack. The men grabbed weapons from the women,
who'd been hiding them under their blankets, and
rushed into the fort, where they massacred most of
the British inhabitants and took some hostage. The
French population was left unharmed.

What is a "Canadian egg roll" in lacrosse?

This is not the postgame snack. Canadian egg roll is slang for a shot where
a player, with the player's back to the net, catches a pass and then swoops
the stick downward in one motion and shoots the ball backward at the net
from knee-height.

ROCKS
AND ROLLS

Why is the game with rocks on ice called "curling," and how did it come to Canada?

The first reference to the game we call curling was recorded in Scotland in 1541 and has nothing to do with the curling path of some stones. The game was, and in many places still is, called "the roaring game" because of the rumbling sound the rocks make while sliding over pebbled ice. This rumbling sound was called a *curr* in the Scots language and is how the game became known as curling. (In the Scots language a *curr* is, among other things, the sound a dove makes when cooing — related to purring.) The word *curling* surfaced in 1620 as the name of the roaring game which would be brought to Canada by Scottish immigrants in the early nineteenth century.

What is "The Brier"?

Called simply "The Brier," the Tim Hortons Brier, which has been sponsored by the doughnut shop chain since 2005, is the annual Canadian men's curling championship, sanctioned by Curling Canada. Since its founding in 1927, the tournament has been sponsored by Macdonald Tobacco (1927–79), Labatt Brewery (1980–2000), and Nokia (2001–04). It is a competition hosting provincial and regional teams, the winner of which goes on to represent Canada at the World Curling Championships.

In 1927 the tournament trophy was called the MacDonald Brier Tankard, after the name of MacDonald's most popular pipe tobacco; *brier* is the name of a plant from which the roots are used to make tobacco smoking pipes. That first Dominion Curling Championship led to the establishment of the Canadian Curling Association in 1935.

Where was the first curling club in Canada?

The first curling club in Canada was formed in Montreal in 1807 by twenty merchants who called themselves the Montreal Curling Club. It has been operating continuously since then and celebrated its two hundredth anniversary in 2007. In 1835 members of the Montreal Curling Club took part in the very first intercity game in Canada, competing against the Quebec Curling Club in the city of Trois-Rivières. Quebec won, and Montreal had to pay for the dinner. Legend has it there was no whisky available, and there were many complaints about having only wine and champagne to drink.

DID YOU KNOW ...
that curling was included in the 1924 Chamonix Winter Olympic Games (men only), but was not an official sport in the Olympic Games again until it was reintroduced at the 1998 Nagano Winter Olympic Games. Since then both Canadian teams have claimed five medals: men's, three gold and two silver, and women's, two gold, one silver, and two bronze.

What is the Tournament of Hearts?

The Scotties Tournament of Hearts is the annual Canadian Women's Curling Championship, sanctioned by the Curling Canada. The winner goes on to represent Canada at the Women's World Curling Championships. The

Tournament of Hearts is a competition hosting provincial teams, although since 1985, the winner gets to return the following years as "Team Canada." The tournament has been sponsored by Kruger Products, a paper manufacturer which makes Scotties tissues, since 1982.

Which Canadian team won the first-ever world curling championship?

- -

The first world curling championship was limited to men and was known as the "Scotch Cup," held in Falkirk and Edinburgh, Scotland, in 1959. The first title was won by the Canadian team from Regina, skipped by Ernie Richardson.

DID YOU KNOW ...
that in early Canada, garrison officers created curling stones called "irons" by filling the metal-rimmed hubs of gun carriages with molten metal and inserting iron handles?

Who was Sandra Schmirler?

- -

When Sandra Schmirler was a kid in Biggar, Saskatchewan, she wanted to play hockey, but since there was no girls' hockey team in town she opted for a broomstick over a hockey stick and took to the curling rink.

She curled all through her school years, and eventually, as an adult, Schmirler would use that broomstick to lead the Canadian women's curling team to gold at the Nagano Winter Olympic Games of 1998 — the first year women's curling appeared in the Olympic Games. Sadly, Sandra Schmirler died of cancer two years later at the age of thirty-six. The Sandra Schmirler MVP Award is presented to the top curler in the playoffs of the Scotties Tournament of Hearts.

MAKING
A SPLASH

Who was the first Canadian to swim the English Channel?

The first Canadian swimmer to accomplish that feat was Winifred "Winnie" Frances Roach-Leuszler of Port Credit, Ontario. On August 16, 1951, the twenty-five-year-old mother of three children completed the swim in thirteen hours and twenty-five minutes. She was within ninety-one metres of shore when a current washed her back 10.5 kilometres, and she had to swim that last exhausting leg all over again. In 1999 Winnie received the Order of Ontario. She was also inducted into the Canadian Armed Forces Sports Hall of Fame and the Ontario Aquatic Hall of Fame. Sadly, Winnie passed away in 2004.

What made Marilyn Bell of Toronto a Canadian icon?

On September 8 and 9, 1954, sixteen-year-old Marilyn Bell became the first person to swim across Lake Ontario. She started at Youngstown, New York, and came ashore twenty hours and fifty-nine minutes later just west of Toronto's CNE grounds at what is now Marilyn Bell Park. The route across the lake was 51.5 kilometres as the crow flies, but due to strong winds and primitive navigational equipment, Marilyn actually had to swim twice that distance. The waves were up to 4.5 metres high, and she was often attacked by lamprey eels. When she finally dragged herself ashore, three hundred thousand cheering people waited to greet her. Over the next two years Bell became the youngest person to swim the English Channel, and she also swam the Juan de Fuca Strait on Canada's West Coast. She has been inducted into Canada's Sports Hall of Fame and the Canadian Aquatics Hall of Fame, and she has been named one of Canada's top athletes of the twentieth century. In 2002 she was awarded the Order of Ontario.

DID YOU KNOW ...

that besides Marilyn Bell, two other women began the cross-Lake Ontario swim on September 8, 1954: Winnie Roach-Leuszler, the first Canadian to swim the English Channel; and American champion long-distance swimmer Florence Chadwick? The Canadian National Exhibition had offered Chadwick a ten thousand dollar prize to swim the lake. Bell considered this a snub of Canadian swimmers, and she took up the challenge with no promise of prize money. Neither Roach-Leuszler nor Chadwick finished the crossing that day.

How many swimming records does Vicki Keith hold?

Vicki Keith of Winnipeg holds sixteen world swimming records and has been the recipient of forty-one honours and awards, including the Order of Canada and the Order of Ontario. Her marathon swimming triumphs have all been part of her efforts to raise money for children with physical disabilities. Keith made her first Lake Ontario crossing in August 1986. One year later she became the first person to make a double crossing of Lake Ontario. In summer 1988 she became the first person to swim across all five Great Lakes: twenty-six kilometres across Lake Erie, seventy-six kilometres across Lake Huron, seventy-two kilometres across Lake Michigan, thirty-two kilometres across Lake Superior, and a thirty-nine-kilometre finale across her favourite swimming hole, Lake Ontario.

TEN VICKI KEITH SWIMMING ACCOMPLISHMENTS

- Most crossings (six) of Lake Ontario.
- First butterfly swim across Lake Ontario.
- First butterfly swim across the English Channel.
- Longest solo swim (distance), 93.3 kilometres.
- Longest solo swim (time), sixty-three hours, forty minutes.
- Continuous swimming (pool), 129 hours, forty-five minutes.
- Longest distance, male or female, butterfly, 78.8 kilometres.
- Circumnavigation of Sydney, Australia, Harbour (butterfly).
- Crossing of Juan de Fuca Strait, British Columbia.
- Crossing of Catalina Channel, California (butterfly).

Which Canadian swimmer has won the most medals at a Summer Olympic Games?

Remarkably, a sixteen-year-old Toronto swimmer by the name of Penny Oleksiak made history at the 2016 Rio Summer Olympic Games, winning two bronze, one silver, and one gold medal in the pool, making her not only the most decorated Canadian swimmer in an Olympic Games, but also the most decorated Canadian Olympian ever in a single Summer Olympic Games. She is also Canada's youngest Olympic gold medallist — and the first born in the twenty-first century! Penny was awarded the Bobbie Rosenfeld Award as Canada's female athlete of the year and the Lou Marsh Trophy as Canada's top athlete in 2016.

OLYMPIC FEATS

What are the most medals ever won by a Canadian at an Olympic Games?

That honour is shared by two Canadian women. At the Torino Winter Olympic Games in 2006, Cindy Klassen became the first Canadian Olympian to win five medals in a single Olympic Games. A short- and long-distance speed skater, Klassen won gold in the 1,500-metre race, silver in the women's team pursuit, silver in the one thousand-metre race, bronze in the three thousand-metre race, and bronze in the five thousand-metre race. When a bronze won at Salt Lake City in 2002 is added to the total, she became the biggest overall medal winner in Canadian Olympic history. But Klassen would soon have to share this distinction with her speed-skating teammate Clara Hughes, who claimed a bronze in the five thousand-metre race at the 2010 Vancouver Winter Olympic Games, bringing her medal total to six also (one gold, one silver, one bronze). Notably, two of Hughes's medals (bronzes) were earned at the Summer Olympic Games, in cycling events.

Which Paralympian was named Canadian athlete of the year in 2008?

In 2008 wheelchair racer Chantal Petitclerc was awarded both the Lou Marsh Trophy and Canadian Press's Bobbie Rosenfeld Award as Canada's female athlete of the year. Petitclerc, who lost the use of both legs in an accident at the age of thirteen, had been competing in the Paralympic Games since 1992. Over five Paralympic Games she amassed an astounding twenty-one medals, including five gold at the 2004 Summer Paralympic Games in Athens. She holds world records in the one hundred-, two hundred-, hour hundred-, eight hundred-, and 1,500-metre distances. A truly inspirational athlete, a municipal ice hockey arena in her hometown of Saint-Marc-des-Carrières now bears her name. Among her many other honours, in 2009 she was given a star on Canada's Walk of Fame and made a Companion of the Order of Canada. On March 18, 2016, Petitclerc was named to the Senate of Canada by Prime Minister Justin Trudeau.

Which Canadian Olympian had a doll created in her image?

Barbara Ann Scott was the first Canadian woman to win an Olympic gold medal in figure skating. After her win at the 1948 Winter Olympic Games in St. Moritz, Switzerland, she returned home to Canada to a hero's welcome. The girl who became known as "Canada's Sweetheart" was thrown a huge civic reception, presented with a new car by the mayor of her hometown of Ottawa (which she had to return in order to retain her amateur athlete status), and honoured by the Reliable Toy Company with the creation of a Barbara Ann Scott doll. She was a great inspiration for many girls born in the late 1940s and 1950s, quite a few of whom had been named after the popular skater.

Why was the score of the first Olympic basketball final between Canada and the United States so low?

Basketball was introduced to the Olympic Games in Berlin in 1936, with teams representing twenty-three countries. By today's standards scores in the tournament were remarkably low. There was good reason for this. The International Basketball Federation, which is the governing body of international basketball, used the 1936 tournament to experiment with outdoor basketball. Rather than cement courts, lawn tennis courts were used for the competition. This caused problems when the weather was adverse, especially during the final game, which was played in a rainstorm. Unable to dribble the ball, players had to be content to play a passing game, and the end result saw the Unites States taking gold over Canada with a score of just 19–8.

Why did Canadian basketball player Irving "Toots" Meretsky not receive his silver medal at the 1936 Summer Olympic Games?

In the first-ever Olympic basketball tournament at the 1936 Summer Olympic Games in Berlin, the Canadian basketball team won silver. It remains the only time a Canadian basketball team has taken a medal at the Olympic Games. But player Irving "Toots" Meretsky, who passed away in 2006, didn't receive a medal at those games because there were nine players on the Canadian squad, and the Berlin officials had only prepared eight medals. It was not until 1996, on the sixtieth anniversary of the Berlin Olympic Games, that his family contacted the IOC, who had a silver medal cast for Toots from the original mould.

Have any Canadians won gold in Olympic boxing?

Canada has seen three boxers emerge from the Olympic ring as gold-medal champions. The first was Bert Schneider, from Montreal, who fought in the welterweight division at the 1920 Summer Olympic Games in Antwerp, Belgium. Schneider defeated four opponents over the space of three days, defeating Britain's Alexander Ireland in the final. The second Canadian gold-winning boxer was Horace "Lefty" Gwynne, from Toronto, who defeated three opponents to take the Olympic bantamweight title at the 1932 Summer Olympic Games in Los Angeles. The third and most famous Canadian gold medallist in boxing is super-heavyweight Lennox "The Lion" Lewis, from Kitchener, Ontario, who took the championship in his division at the 1988 Seoul Summer Olympic Games. Lewis went on to win the professional world heavyweight title in 1993. Sadly, up to and including the 2016 Summer Olympic Games, Canada has not medalled in the sport since 1996.

How did Canadian cyclist Clara Hughes win gold at the Winter Olympic Games?

Canadian cyclist Clara Hughes made her Olympic debut competing in the road race and time trail competition at the 1996 Summer Olympic Games in Atlanta. She took bronze in both events, finishing the 104.4-kilometre road race just thirty-one one-hundredths of a second behind French gold medallist Jeannie Longo-Ciprelli. In 2001 Hughes took up speed skating, and after just seven weeks of training, she made the Canadian team and accompanied them to the 2002 Winter Olympic Games in Salt Lake City, where she garnered bronze in the five thousand-metre race. But she wasn't done yet. Hughes donned the skates once more for the Turin Summer Olympic Games in 2006, where she upgraded her medal standing, first to silver, coming in second with fellow Canucks in the team pursuit, and then to gold, finishing a full second ahead of the pack in the five thousand-metre race. As mentioned earlier she is tied with speed skater Cindy Klassen as the Canadian with the most Olympic medals — six in total.

Since her retirement from Olympic competition, Hughes has received many honours: a school in Oshawa, Ontario, was renamed for her; she was named to both the Order of Manitoba and as an Officer of the Order of Canada; she received a star on the Canada's Walk of Fame; and she was inducted into Canada's Sports Hall of Fame. Today Hughes is very active in charitable organizations like Right to Play, and she is also the national spokesperson for the Bell Let's Talk mental health initiative.

Why was Canadian equestrian Eric Lamaze twice banned from Olympic competition for life?

Show jumper Eric Lamaze had a wild ride getting to Olympic gold. Prior to the 1996 Summer Olympic Games in Atlanta, Lamaze tested positive for cocaine use and was disqualified from competition. In July 2000, prior to the Sydney Summer Olympic Games, he tested positive for use of the banned substances pseudoephedrine and ephedrine. Under Olympic rules, the second strike brought an automatic lifetime suspension. But the ban would not stick. The pseudoephedrine, which came from an Advil cold remedy, was not enough alone to warrant a ban. And the ephedrine, it turned out, had been an unlisted ingredient in a dietary supplement Lamaze had used. Because he didn't know he'd taken it, the ban was lifted that August. But when Lamaze tested again a few days later, cocaine was once again found in his system, and the Canadian Centre for Ethics in Sport slapped him with his second lifetime ban. Through arbitration Lamaze was eventually reinstated, and at the Beijing Summer Olympic Games in 2008 he finally got his Olympic chance. He brought home silver in the team jumping competition and gold in the individual.

Have Canadians ever won gold in Olympic gymnastics?

Canada's overall medal count in Olympic gymnastics stands at fourteen, four of which are gold. At the 1984 Los Angeles Summer Olympic Games, Vancouver-born Lori Fung became not only Canada's first gold medallist in gymnastics, but she also became the first-ever medal recipient in rhythmic gymnastics, which were being contested for the first time at those Olympic Games. Canada had to wait twenty years for the next gymnastics gold, which was won by Kyle Keith Shewfelt in the floor exercise at the 2004 Summer Olympic Games in Athens. Since trampoline was added to the gymnastics mix in 2000, Canadians have excelled at the sport, winning seven medals over the years, including two golds for Rosie MacLennan at the 2012 and 2016 Summer Olympic Games.

Why did Canadian rower Silken Laumann almost miss the 1992 Summer Olympic Games?

Prior to the 1992 Summer Olympic Games in Barcelona, Canadian rower Silken Laumann was seen as a strong contender to win gold in the single sculls race. But on May 15 of that year, while training, her shell was involved in a collision with the boat of German coxless pair team Colin von Ettinghausen and Peter Hoeltzenbein. The collision resulted in horrible wounds to Laumann's leg that required five operations and weeks in hospital. Doctors doubted she would be able to row at world-class levels again, but Laumann was determined to prove them wrong and by late June she was back on the water training. Even with her leg severely weakened, Laumann managed to win a bronze medal in the single sculls event in Barcelona on July 28. She achieved silver in the event four years later in Atlanta.

DID YOU KNOW ...
that Canada's only Olympic medal in tennis was won in 2000 by Daniel Nestor and Sébastien Lareau at the men's doubles tournament in Sydney? They took gold, defeating Aussies Todd Woodbridge and Mark Woodforde in the final.

DID YOU KNOW ...
that when Canadian Simon Whitfield arrived at the 2000 Sydney Summer Olympic Games to compete in the first-ever Olympic triathlon — which he would go on to win — he was ranked just thirteenth in the world in the sport?

Which Canadian women have won Olympic medals in wrestling?

Women's wrestling made its debut at the 2004 Summer Olympic Games in Athens, where Canada's Tonya Verbeek won silver in the fifty-five-kilogram freestyle event. At the 2008 Beijing Summer Olympic Games, Verbeek again medalled, taking bronze in the same weight class. She competed in her third Olympic Games in 2012, and she brought home another silver medal. Meanwhile, also at Beijing, Canadian Carol Huynh, competing in the forty-eight-kilogram class, won Canada's first Olympic gold in women's wrestling. Huynh also picked up a bronze in 2012 (appropriately, Huynh's last name is pronounced "win"!). Most recently, in Rio in 2016, Erica Wiebe won gold in the seventy-five-kilogram class. So in total, Canadian women have picked up six medals in the sport — two gold, two silver, and two bronze.

How did the Canadian women's biathlon team raise money to train for the 2010 Winter Olympic Games?

The five-member Canadian women's biathlon team, in need of funding to attend the 2010 Vancouver Winter Olympic Games, issued a 2009 wall calendar that featured "tasteful" nude photos of themselves posing with their rifles.

DID YOU KNOW ...
that the first Canadian Olympic ice hockey team,
which played at the first Winter Olympic Games in
Chamonix, France, in 1924, won gold with only three
goals scored against it in the entire tournament? In
fact, in the Canucks' first three matches, they scored
eighty-five times without conceding a goal!

What object did a Canadian bury at centre ice in 2002 at the Salt Lake City Winter Olympic Games?

A Canadian named Trent Evans from Edmonton took care of the ice at
Salt Lake City's E Center during the Winter Olympic Games in 2002.
When he noticed there was no dot to indicate where to drop the puck for
faceoffs, he buried a Canadian dollar coin, a loonie, under the ice at the
centre ice faceoff circle and obscured it with some yellow paint. Both the
Canadian women's and men's hockey teams were told about the good luck
charm, but were asked not to breathe a word about it. Canada went on to
win gold in both men's and women's hockey. After the medals were won,
Wayne Gretzky, executive director of the Canadian men's team, held a
press conference and pulled the loonie out of his jacket pocket, telling the
assembled, "We took it out of the ice tonight, and we're going to present
it to the Hall of Fame. We got two gold medals out of it. That's pretty
special." Strangely enough, at the 2006 Winter Olympic Games a loonie
wasn't buried at centre ice. In those games Canada's men's hockey team
failed to get any medal, though the women's team did strike gold. Loonies
were buried in the ice at the Olympic curling competition that year, and
the Canadian men's team grabbed gold.

Which Canadian runner broke a world record in the 100-metre and won gold at the 1996 Summer Olympic Games in Atlanta?

- -

Donovan Bailey won the 100-metre race and a gold medal, setting a world record of 9.84 seconds. He and his teammates, Robert Esmie, Glenroy Gilbert, and Bruny Surin, then went on to win another gold in the men's four by 100-metre relay at the same Olympic Games.

Which Canadian sprinter became a star at the 2016 Rio Summer Olympic Games?

- -

Markham, Ontario's Andre De Grasse wowed Canadian crowds in Rio when he won three medals — a silver and two bronze — in the 200-metre, 100-metre, and four by 100-metre men's relay, respectively. De Grasse is the first Canadian sprinter to win three medals in a single Olympic Games. The young sprinter garnered much media attention when he cruised up alongside world-record-holder Usain Bolt in their 200-metre semifinal and flashed the tall Jamaican a wide grin. The much smaller, five-foot-nine De Grasse looked like he could be the legend's younger brother, and when Bolt flashed a wide smile back at his Canadian challenger, the media went wild. De Grasse was voted Canada's male athlete of the year for 2016 (Postmedia).

Which Canadian won gold at the 2016 Rio Summer Olympic Games, the first to do so in his sport in more than eighty years?

Canadian Derek Drouin's first place finish in high jump at the 2016 Rio Summer Olympic Games was the first gold-medal win for Canada in a field sport since 1932, when Duncan McNaughton took home the top medal, also for the high jump, at the Summer Olympic Games in Los Angeles.

MORE
CHAMPIONS
OF CANADIAN
SPORT

Who was the best Canadian female athlete of the first half of the twentieth century?

Voted the best Canadian female athlete in the first half of the twentieth century, Fanny "Bobbie" Rosenfeld was an exceptional multi-sport performer. Born in Russia she came to Canada as an infant. By the early 1920s she excelled at track and field, and when women were finally allowed to compete in the Summer Olympic Games in 1928, she was part of the Canadian team in Amsterdam. Rosenfeld won a silver medal in the one hundred-metre sprint and was the lead runner on the four hundred-metre relay team, which won a gold medal in a record time of 48.2 seconds. The fleet-of-foot athlete also held Canadian records in the running and standing broad jump and in the discus, not to mention once clocking a world-record eleven seconds in the 100-yard dash. Rosenfeld was also a pretty good softball player. But hockey, she claimed, was her first love, and she was a standout on various teams in Ontario throughout the 1920s and early 1930s. Some of her best hockey was played for the Toronto Patterson St. Pats in the Ladies' Ontario Hockey Association. A *Toronto Star* reporter in the 1920s had this to say about Rosenfeld and the St. Pats after watching a game: "In Bobbie Rosenfeld and Casey McLean, the Pats have two players who could earn a place on any OHA (men's) junior team. Both are speedy and good stickhandlers and pack a shot that has plenty of steam on it." Increasingly crippled by arthritis in the early 1930s, Rosenfeld finally retired from all competitive sports and became a sports columnist for Toronto's *Globe and Mail*. In 1949 she was inducted into Canada's Sports Hall of Fame.

Who were voted Canada's top ten female athletes of the twentieth century?

(from a 1999 survey of newspaper editors and broadcasters conducted by the Canadian Press and Broadcast News):

1. Nancy Greene (born 1943), skier
2. Silken Laumann (born 1964), rower
3. Barbara Ann Scott (1928–2012), figure skater
4. Myriam Bédard (born 1969), biathlete
5. Marnie McBean (born 1968), rower
6. Fanny "Bobbie" Rosenfeld (1904–69), track and field (voted female athlete of the first half of the twentieth century)
7. Catriona Le May Doan (born 1970), speed skater
8. Sandra Post (born 1948), golfer
9. Marilyn Bell (born 1937), long-distance swimmer
10. Elaine Tanner (born 1951), swimmer

Who were voted Canada's top ten male athletes of the twentieth century?

(from a 1999 survey of newspaper editors and broadcasters conducted by the Canadian Press and Broadcast News):

1. Wayne Gretzky (born 1961), ice hockey player
2. Gordie Howe (1928–2016), ice hockey player
3. Bobby Orr (born 1948), ice hockey player

4. Lionel Conacher (1901–54), multi-sport athlete (voted male athlete of the first half of the twentieth century)
5. Maurice Richard (1921–2000), ice hockey player
6. Donovan Bailey (born 1967), track and field
7. Ferguson Jenkins (born 1943), baseball player
8. Mario Lemieux (born 1965), ice hockey player
9. Larry Walker (born 1966), baseball player
10. Gaétan Boucher (born 1958), speed skater

What is the oldest operating golf club in Canada?

The Royal Montreal Golf Club, founded in 1873, holds the title of the oldest operating golf course in not just Canada, but also in all of North America. Eleven years after its creation, the club received a patronage from Queen Victoria. Originally a nine-hole course in Fletcher's Field, part of Mount Royal Park, the club moved in 1896 to Dixie, in the parish of Dorval, and then to its current location on Île-Bizard in 1959, where forty-five holes were constructed.

How many Canadians have won major golf championships?

The tournaments that have been designated majors, in both men's and women's golf, have varied over the years. But since the beginning of all major tournaments, only five Canadians have managed to rise to the champion ranks. In 2003 Mike Weir, of Sarnia, Ontario, delighted his country by donning the green jacket at the Masters. In 1971 and 1966 Gary Cowan of

Kitchener, Ontario, won the United States Amateur Championship. Ross "Sandy" Somerville of London, Ontario, also took that tournament in 1932.

In the women's field, Canada has produced two winners of the LPGA Championship: Sandra Post, of Oakville, Ontario, did it in 1968. And in 2016 eighteen-year-old Brooke Henderson did it with a victory in a sudden death playoff at the KPMG Women's PGA Championship in Washington State.

Which was the first golf club to admit women members in North America?

The Royal Montreal, in Quebec, holds many notable records, including being the longest continuously running course in North America and the first course to employ a club professional (Englishman Willie Davis), but perhaps its most notable achievement was to be the first course in North America to admit women members, in 1891.

Which Canadian invented five-pin bowling?

In 1905 a pool-hall owner named Thomas F. "Tommy" Ryan decided to install Canada's first "regulation" ten-pin alley in a second storey above a jewellery store in downtown Toronto. The ten-lane establishment, known as the Toronto Bowling Club, resembled a southern plantation, with potted palm trees, ceiling fans, string orchestra, piano, and an immense lunch counter. In 1909, responding to customer complaints about the size and weight of the ten-pin balls, Ryan had his father turn down five of the larger pins on a lathe, to approximately three-quarters of their original size. He then spaced five of these pins equally on the ninety-one-centimetre ten-pin triangle. Ryan took a hand-size hard rubber ball — approximately thirteen centimetres in diameter and 1.6 kilograms in weight — and rolled it down the ten-pin lane to invent five-pin bowling. In 1912 he added rubber rings to the pins.

Which Canadian was the first runner to win back-to-back Boston Marathons?

Canadian runner John Caffrey was the first person to win back-to-back Boston Marathons. He led the pack in 1900, with a time of 2:39:44, and in 1901, with a time of 2:29:23. Both times were course records.

How did Tom Longboat astound the world in 1907?

Tom Longboat was an Onondaga from the Six Nations Reserve near Brantford, Ontario. In 1907 he became the first aboriginal long-distance runner to win the Boston Marathon. He ran the thirty-nine kilometre course in a record-breaking 2:24:24. He had beaten the previous record by an incredible four minutes and fifty-nine seconds. The following year Longboat collapsed during the Olympic marathon. Nonetheless, he went on to have a distinguished professional career as a runner.

?

DID YOU KNOW ...
that in spite of his athletic accomplishments, Tom Longboat often experienced the ugliness of racism? He was frequently subjected to racial smears in the press. When his running career ended, he worked as a street cleaner in Toronto.

Has any Canadian ever worn the yellow jersey in the Tour de France?

Two of the three Canadians who have appeared in the Tour de France have worn the yellow jersey. Steve Bauer rode in eleven tours and pulled on the yellow jersey twice, both times in the 1988 race. That year Bauer led the tour on day two and also on days 8–11. The other Canadian to wear yellow was Alex Stieda, who led the tour on its second day in 1986. No Canadian has ever won the famed race, however.

What are alley cat races?

Started in Toronto in 1989, urban bicycle messengers began organizing unsanctioned bicycle races in the downtown cores of major North American cities. They call these events alley cat races. These checkpoint-to-checkpoint races have very few rules or regulations. They culminate, in part, each year with the annual Cycle Messenger World Championships, which started in 1993 and continue today, taking place in a different city each year — Toronto hosted in 1995 and 2008, Edmonton in 2004, and Montreal is scheduled to host in 2017. In addition to a three-hour street race, events include three hundred-metre sprints, a cargo race (in which competitors carry heavy packages), bunny-hopping over a bar, bike polo, track stand (where cyclists try to maintain a stationary position for as long as possible while on a bicycle), skids, and more.

Who were the Crazy Canucks?

The Crazy Canucks was a group of Canadian ski racers who competed in the 1970s and 1980s. "Jungle" Jim Hunter, Dave Irwin, Dave Murray, Steve Podborski, and Ken Read earned their nickname due to the fast, seemingly reckless style of skiing they employed in the downhill events in which they competed. The group was given a star on Canada's Walk of Fame in 2006. The only other skier with a star on the walk is the legendary Nancy Greene.

DID YOU KNOW ...

? that the first ski-hill rope tow was invented by Alex Foster in 1931 and installed at "The Big Hill" in Shawbridge, Quebec, north of Montreal? It was powered by a Dodge automobile, jacked up on blocks, with a rope looped around a wheel rim. A ride up the hill cost five cents.

Who was the first Canadian heavyweight boxing champion of the world?

Tommy Burns (born Noah Brusso in Normandy Township, Ontario, June 17, 1881) was an up-and-coming middleweight boxer in 1905, anxious for a shot at the middleweight title. Marvin Hart inherited the world heavyweight title when champion James Jeffries retired from the ring. Hart was obliged to defend his new title, and he chose Burns as his first challenger, expecting an easy victory. At five foot seven, and 79 kilograms, Burns was considered too small to be classed as a heavyweight contender. Nonetheless, he won a decision over Hart in a twenty-round bout in Los Angeles on February 23, 1906. In a period of less than two years, Burns successfully defended his title eleven times, always against much bigger opponents and usually winning by knockout. In San Diego he took on two challengers in one night, and he knocked both out in the first round. Burns defended his title in the United States, Great Britain, France, and Australia.

How did Canadian boxer George Chuvalo restore legitimacy to professional boxing?

In 1966 professional boxing was reeling from several body blows. Muhammad Ali (Cassius Clay) had won a pair of controversial victories over Sonny Liston, and there were accusations that the fights had been fixed. The American Legion, incensed over Ali's refusal to be inducted into the military on the grounds of being a conscientious objector, threatened to boycott any American city that hosted an Ali fight. Ernie Terrell, with whom Ali was scheduled to have his next bout, backed out. Ali was offered a bout in Toronto with George Chuvalo, the heavyweight champion of Canada. Boxing fans anticipated an easy victory for Ali, who up to that point had been winning all of his fights by knockout or TKO. Instead, Ali found himself in a hard battle with an opponent who just wouldn't go down. Ali won the match by decision, but later said that Chuvalo was the toughest opponent he had ever faced. Chuvalo's gutsy performance earned him, and professional boxing, a whole new respect.

What is the Canadian connection between Muhammad Ali and Mike Tyson?

When Mike Tyson won his first heavyweight championship bout in November 1986, he took the title from Jamaican-Canadian fighter Trevor Berbick, who had only been WBC heavyweight champion since March 22, 1986. Five years prior, on December 11, 1981, Berbick had been the last fighter to face Muhammad Ali in the ring before Ali retired. The twenty-six-year-old Berbick defeated Ali, thirty-nine, by a unanimous decision. Berbick remains the only Canadian to have held a world heavyweight title.

Which Canadian Formula One champion followed in his father's footsteps?

Gilles Villeneuve won six Formula One Grand Prix races before he was killed in an on-track accident in 1982. His son Jacques has won the CART Championship (1995), the Indianapolis 500 (1995), and the Formula One World Championship (1997).

AFTERWORD

Doug Lennox's contribution to Canada was immense, and it is entirely fitting that this compilation of his work coincides with the country's 150th birthday. This is the work of a prodigiously talented man with a unique insight into the country's history and culture.

Now You Know Canada is an eclectic book, jammed with fascinating details about the country it celebrates. In this respect, it mirrors its author, a man of protean abilities and a renaissance man in every sense of the word. Over the course of his life, Doug touched upon many aspects of the Canadian experience. From his early military service with the United Nations to a long and prolific career with the CBC, his life was quintessentially Canadian.

As a radio producer, Doug celebrated our culture and history. As an actor, he contributed to a broad array of our film and television projects. As a writer, he chronicled diverse facets of the country, many of them on display in this remarkable publication.

One of Canada's most enduring character actors, Doug's face was recognizable to generations of Canadians. Within the arts community, he was something of a legend, with credits on more than eighty film and television productions, including *The New Avengers*, *Police Academy*, and the X-Men films.

Doug's radio programs included award-winning productions such as *Touch the Earth*, *Vanishing Century*, and *Journey to the 20th Century*, many of which he wrote, produced, and voiced. Over the course of his career he worked with a who's who of iconic Canadian talent, including Juliette Cavazzi, Sylvia Tyson, and Anne Murray. His long-running syndicated radio show *Now You Know* gave birth to his career as an author of the immensely successful book series of the same name. *Now You Know Canada* is the latest in this best-selling franchise, which — like so much of Doug's work — reflects his deep affection for, and broad appreciation of, everything the country stands for.

As Canada celebrates its sesquicentennial, this is the perfect time for a book like *Now You Know Canada*, because there is something very serious about trivia. These are the details that make up our national character and our cultural DNA. They constitute a lively mix of history and whimsy, biography and geography. One cannot read this book without learning new things, which is exactly how Doug would have wanted it.

It's hard to see the publication of *Now You Know Canada* and not wish Doug were here to celebrate it with us. But writers undertake their calling in the knowledge that if they are fortunate their words will live after them. For Doug Lennox, this publication is further evidence of his talent and another chapter in a long and broad engagement with Canadian culture. This book, like so much of Doug's work, stands testament to his abiding love of Canada and his legacy as a consummate Canadian.

Jean-Marie Heimrath
Executive Producer and Friend

QUESTION
AND
FEATURE LIST

O CANADA !

Who gave the word *Canadian* its modern meaning?, 8

What is the official motto of Canada?, 8

What does *True North* mean in the English version of the anthem "O Canada"?, 9

How big is Canada's newest territory?, 9

Why are the colours of Canada red and white?, 10

Why was the maple leaf chosen as the national badge of Canada?, 11

When was our national anthem "O Canada" first played?, 12

Who were the leading Fathers of Confederation?, 12

When did Canada officially become its own country?, 13

How did the city of Calgary get its name?, 13

How did Niagara Falls get its name?, 14

Who was the first Niagara Falls daredevil?, 14

Who was the first person to go over Niagara Falls in a barrel?, 15

Where did the term "Canuck" come from?, 16

POLICY-MAKERS AND GROUND-BREAKERS

Why was Sir Wilfrid Laurier considered one of Canada's greatest prime
  ministers?, 18

Why was Lester Pearson awarded the Nobel Prize?, 18

How did Lincoln Alexander make Canadian history?, 19

Who was the first black woman to run for the leadership of a Canadian national political party?, 19

Who was the first black woman elected to Canada's Parliament?, 20

Who was the first aboriginal Canadian elected to a provincial legislature in Canada?, 21

Feature: Other Firsts for First Nations Politicians, 21

Who was Canada's first female member of Parliament?, 21

Feature: Leading the Way: Other Female Firsts in Canadian Politics, 22

Who was Mary Ann Shadd?, 23

Who were the Famous Five?, 24

Feature: Individual accomplishments of the Famous Five, 24

Who was the first woman appointed to the Supreme Court of Canada?, 25

REBELLIONS

Who was the leader of the 1837–38 Rebellion in Upper Canada?, 27

How did the Family Compact respond to Mackenzie's attacks in the *Colonial Advocate*?, 27

Why did Mackenzie turn to armed insurrection?, 28

Where did the main engagement of the Mackenzie Rebellion take place?, 28

What was the aftermath of the Mackenzie Rebellion?, 29

Why is Louis Riel considered the founder of Manitoba?, 29

Why did Riel have to flee from Manitoba?, 30

Who was Riel charged with killing?, 30

What happened to Riel after the Red River Rebellion?, 31

Why did Riel return to Canada?, 31

Who was Gabriel Dumont?, 32

How did Riel's return to Canada lead to rebellion?, 32

Where did the main battle of the Northwest Rebellion take place?, 33

What happened to Dumont and Riel?, 33

CANADA AT WAR

Why does Vimy Ridge have a special place in Canadian military history?, 35

What happened at Passchendaele?, 35

Feature: Ten Canadians Awarded the Victoria Cross After Passchendaele, 36

Who was the top Canadian air ace in the First World War?, 36

What type of plane did Billy Bishop fly?, 37

What Canadian fighter pilot was credited with killing the Red Baron?, 38

Who was the most decorated Canadian in the First World War?, 38

What distinction did the Royal Newfoundland Regiment have in the First World War?, 39

Why is August 19, 1942, considered one of the darkest days in Canadian military history?, 39

What was "The Devil's Brigade"?, 40

Which Canadian was the real "Tunnel King" in the true story of the Great Escape?, 40

How did a cigarette case save the life of *Star Trek*'s "Scotty" during the Normandy Campaign?, 41

How did a Canadian fighter pilot knock Germany's top general out of the war?, 42

What is the "Diefenbunker"?, 43

How many Canadians served in the Korean War?, 43

Where is Canada's Highway of Heroes?, 44

HEROES AND LEGENDS

Who was Big Joe Mufferaw?, 46

Who was the Cape Breton Giant?, 46

Who was Klondike Joe Boyle?, 47

Why is "Wild Goose Jack" a hero to conservationists?, 48

Why is Sir Wilfred Grenfell fondly remembered in Newfoundland and Labrador?, 48

What is the motto of the RCMP?, 49

Who was Sam Steele?, 49

Who was the Angel of Long Point?, 50

What great height did Sharon Wood reach?, 51

How did Clara Brett Martin challenge the Law Society of Upper Canada?, 51

PRODIGIES OF SCIENCE, INVENTION, AND MEDICINE

Why are David Fife and Charles Saunders heroes to western Canadian wheat growers?, 54

Which Canadian is known as the Father of Standard Time?, 54

Who was Canada's first female doctor?, 55

How did Dr. Frederick Banting of Ontario astound American business-men?, 56

Where in Canada was Pablum invented?, 57

What may have been Alexander Graham Bell's motivation for inventing the telephone?, 58

CANADIAN DISASTERS

What was the deadliest man-made disaster in Canada's history?, 60

How did Hurricane Hazel take the lives of five Toronto firemen?, 60

Who were the heroes of Canada's worst maritime disaster?, 61

How did a projectionist and an usher become heroes during Canada's worst movie theatre fire?, 62

Who was "Eddy," and how did he help save dozens from a terrible shipboard fire in Toronto Harbour?, 63

INTREPID EXPLORERS

How do we know the Vikings were the first Europeans to explore the East Coast of Canada?, 65

Who was John Cabot?, 65

What were Jacques Cartier's accomplishments?, 66

Why is Samuel de Champlain called "The Father of New France" and "The Father of Acadia"?, 67

How did Champlain make the Iroquois the arch-enemies of New France?, 67

Who was "the Columbus of the Great Lakes"?, 68

What was the most infamous mutiny in Canadian history?, 68

Why did Henry Hudson's crew mutiny?, 68

Who was known as "The Man Who Mapped the West"?, 69

What important scientific discovery was made by Arctic explorer James Clark Ross?, 70

When did the first ship successfully navigate the Northwest Passage?, 71

What famous explorer played hockey in the Arctic?, 71

What is the mystery of Franklin's expedition?, 72

How did Franklin get the moniker "the man who ate his boots"?, 72

Who was the first Canadian astronaut?, 73

Who was the first Canadian woman in space?, 73

ENTERTAIN ME

Which Canadian actress was known as "America's Sweetheart"?, 76

What is Canada's longest running one-hour TV drama?, 76

What is the longest running Canadian comedy-drama series of all time?, 77

Who are the only two Canadians who have won the Nobel Prize for Literature?, 78

How did a Canadian bear become the inspiration for A.A. Milne's Winnie-the-Pooh?, 79

What popular board game was created by Canadians?, 79

What is the bestselling album by a Canadian artist of all time?, 80

THE OLD BALL GAME

Which Canadian professional sports team played their first major league game in the snow?, 82

Where was the first retractable dome stadium in Canada?, 82

How many pitchers for Canadian baseball teams have thrown a perfect game?, 83

What was the first non-American team in the major leagues?, 83

Who is Youppi!?, 84

Who did the Montreal Expos face in their first and last games?, 84

Why did the Expos unfurl a banner commemorating their 1994 team at their final home game?, 85

How did the Toronto Blue Jays get their name?, 85

What is the highest-scoring game in World Series history?, 86

Has the MLB All-Star game ever been played outside the United States?, 86

GRIDIRON HISTORY

Who was the Grey Cup named after?, 88

How many American cities have fielded teams in the Canadian Football League (CFL)?, 89

What was the most successful American team in the CFL?, 89

What CFL team played without a name during its first season?, 90

Who came first, the Ottawa Rough Riders or the Saskatchewan Roughriders?, 90

How many times has the CFL staged an All-Star Game?, 91

How many Eastern Division Championships have the Winnipeg Blue Bombers won?, 92

What major brewery named its most popular beer after a football team?, 93

Who owned both the Hamilton Tiger-Cats and the Toronto Maple Leafs?, 94

How many teams have gone undefeated in a CFL season?, 94

How many incarnations of the Montreal Alouettes have there been?, 95

What Canadian university football team was part of U.S. college football until 2002?, 96

How did the Hamilton Tiger-Cats get the hyphenated name?, 96

What Canadian football player was the coveted trophy in a season of *The Bachelor?, 97*

Why is a touchdown worth six points?, 97

When was instant replay introduced as a means of reviewing calls in the CFL?, 98

What is a "rouge" in Canadian football?, 98

Why is Canadian football considered a "passing" game while American football is considered a "running" game?, 99

Who is the CFL's all-time pass king?, 100

Who is the only player elected to both the Pro Football Hall of Fame and the Canadian Football Hall of Fame?, 100

Which CFL player was known as "The Little General"?, 101

Who passed up an opportunity to interview for a Rhodes Scholarship in order to play in the CFL?, 101

Who declared, "It will take an act of God to beat us on Saturday" prior to a 1969 CFL playoff game?, 102

Who did the Calgary Stampeders ban from a playoff game against the Saskatchewan Roughriders in 2006?, 102

What was memorable about the 1948 Grey Cup?, 103

Which team has won the most Grey Cups?, 103

When was the first Grey Cup played?, 104

When was the first Vanier Cup played?, 104

Who has won the most Vanier Cups?, 105

What Canadian player has scored the most points in the CFL?, 105

Who is the coach with the most wins in CFL history?, 105

Where was the one hundredth Grey Cup game played?, 106

Feature: The Super Six: Greatest Grey Cup Plays, 107

CANADA'S GAME

Who made the first hockey sticks?, 111

Why is Kingston, Ontario, thought by many to be the birthplace of hockey?, 112

When was the first organized hockey team founded in Canada?, 112

What teams were involved in the world's first hockey championship?, 113

When was the first game in the National Hockey League played?, 113

Who is Peter Puck?, 114

What is the best children's story ever written about hockey?, 115

Who wrote the theme song for CBC-TV's *Hockey Night in Canada*?, 115

Which Canadian invented tabletop hockey?, 116

When did "Coach's Corner" debut on *Hockey Night in Canada*?, 116

When was hockey first broadcast on television in Canada?, 117

Which Canadian first said, "He shoots, he scores!"?, 118

Who was the first Canadian hockey player to grace the cover of *Sports Illustrated*?, 118

Where did the nickname "Habs" come from to describe the Montreal Canadiens?, 119

Which Canadian player holds the most records in the NHL?, 120

Which Canadian holds the NHL record for scoring the most goals in one game?, 121

What was the highest-scoring game in NHL history?, 121

Which NHL player has won the most scoring titles?, 122

Who holds the NHL record for the most points in one game?, 122

What Canadian holds the record for the most goals in a single NHL season by a defenceman?, 123

What Canadian NHL player holds the record for the most fifty-goal seasons?, 124

Which Canadian was the first NHL player to score one hundred points in a regular season?, 124

Which Canadian player was the first to score more than five hundred NHL goals in his career?, 125

Which Canadian player is the only rookie to win the NHL scoring championship?, 126

Which Canadian goaltender has won the most NHL regular-season games?, 127

Which Canadian goalie has the most playoff victories?, 127

What Canadian goalie has recorded the most regular-season shutouts in the NHL?, 128

Which Canadian was the first goaltender in the NHL to wear a mask?, 128

Which Canadian NHL player was the first to wear a helmet?, 129

Which Canadian NHL player was the last to play without a helmet?, 129

Which Canadian was the first black player to see ice time in the NHL?, 130

Who was the first full-blooded aboriginal player in the NHL?, 131

What kind of car was Tim Horton driving when he was killed?, 132

What NHL superstar was offered the position of governor general of Canada?, 133

When and where in Canada was the first official NHL All-Star Game played?, 134

What led to the Richard riots in Montreal?, 135

What actually killed Howie Morenz, the Montreal Canadiens' first superstar?, 136

Where in Canada was the first NHL game played outdoors?, 137

What Canadian Hall of Fame hockey player only had one eye?, 138

What incredible feat did Mario Lemieux accomplish on New Year's Eve
1988?, 139

Which unlikely opponent beat Canada's hockey team in the gold-medal
match at the 1936 Winter Olympics?, 140

Which Canadian scored the first goal and assisted on the last goal of the
1972 Canada–Soviet Union Summit Series?, 140

Who were the first three Canadians to join the "Triple Gold Club"?, 142

What did Canadian Abigail Hoffman do that caused an international
furor?, 143

When was the first Women's World Hockey Championship held?, 144

Which Canadian was the first woman to play in the NHL?, 144

Feature: Six Top Canadian Women's Hockey Players, 145

THE BEAUTIFUL GAME ... NOW IN CANADA

What is the Voyageurs Cup?, 148

Has Canada ever won a major international soccer tournament?, 148

What two records did Canadian Kara Lang set when she was just fifteen
years old?, 149

What was the first Canadian Major League Soccer team?, 150

Which Canadian soccer player has scored the most international goals?, 150

SCOOPS ON CANADIAN HOOPS

Which Canadian invented basketball?, 152

What Canadian team lost the first NBA game?, 152

Why did Toronto Raptors fans wear baby bibs printed with the number 15
on April 15, 2005?, 153

Who was the first Canadian to be selected first overall in an NBA draft?, 153

Who is the most successful Canadian to ever play in the NBA?, 154

CANADA'S OTHER NATIONAL GAME

What is *baaga'adowe*?, 156

Who invented lacrosse?, 156

Why is lacrosse called *lacrosse?*, 157
What were early lacrosse sticks and balls made of?, 157
What is a modern lacrosse ball made of?, 158
What is a "Canadian egg roll" in lacrosse? 159

ROCKS AND ROLLS
Why is the game with rocks on ice called "curling," and how did it come
    to Canada?, 161
What is "The Brier"?, 161
Where was the first curling club in Canada?, 162
What is the Tournament of Hearts?, 162
Which Canadian team won the first-ever world curling championship?, 163
Who was Sandra Schmirler?, 163

MAKING A SPLASH
Who was the first Canadian to swim the English Channel?, 166
What made Marilyn Bell of Toronto a Canadian icon?, 166
How many swimming records does Vicki Keith hold?, 167
Feature: Ten Vicki Keith Swimming Accomplishments, 168
Which Canadian swimmer has won the most medals at a Summer Olympic
    Games?, 168

OLYMPIC FEATS
What are the most medals ever won by a Canadian at an Olympic
    Games?, 170
Which Paralympian was named Canadian athlete of the year in 2008?, 170
Which Canadian Olympian had a doll created in her image?, 171
Why was the score of the first Olympic basketball final between Canada and
    the United States so low?, 171
Why did Canadian basketball player Irving "Toots" Meretsky not receive his
    silver medal at the 1936 Summer Olympic Games?, 172
Have any Canadians won gold in Olympic boxing?, 173

How did Canadian cyclist Clara Hughes win gold at the Winter Olympic Games?, 173

Why was Canadian equestrian Eric Lamaze twice banned from Olympic competition for life?, 174

Have Canadians ever won gold in Olympic gymnastics?, 175

Why did Canadian rower Silken Laumann almost miss the 1992 Summer Olympic Games?, 176

Which Canadian women have won Olympic medals in wrestling?, 177

How did the Canadian women's biathlon team raise money to train for the 2010 Winter Olympic Games?, 177

What object did a Canadian bury at centre ice in 2002 at the Salt Lake City Winter Olympic Games?, 178

Which Canadian runner broke a world record in the one-hundred-metre and won gold at the 1996 Summer Olympic Games in Atlanta?, 179

Which Canadian sprinter became a star at the 2016 Rio Summer Olympic Games?, 179

Which Canadian won gold at the 2016 Rio Summer Olympic Games, the first to do so in his sport in more than eighty years?, 180

MORE CHAMPIONS OF CANADIAN SPORT

Who was the best Canadian female athlete of the first half of the twentieth century?, 182

Who were voted Canada's top ten female athletes of the twentieth century?, 183

Who were voted Canada's top ten male athletes of the twentieth century?, 183

What is the oldest operating golf club in Canada?, 184

How many Canadians have won major golf championships?, 184

Which was the first golf club to admit women members in North America?, 185

Which Canadian invented five-pin bowling?, 185

Which Canadian was the first runner to win back-to-back Boston Marathons?, 186

How did Tom Longboat astound the world in 1907?, 186

Has any Canadian ever worn the yellow jersey in the Tour de France?, 187

What are alley cat races?, 188

Who were the Crazy Canucks?, 188

Who was the first Canadian heavyweight boxing champion of the world?, 189

How did Canadian boxer George Chuvalo restore legitimacy to professional boxing?, 190

What is the Canadian connection between Muhammad Ali and Mike Tyson?, 190

Which Canadian Formula One champion followed in his father's footsteps?, 191